Paint Ideas & Projects

FROM THE EDITORS OF **This Old House**

Contents

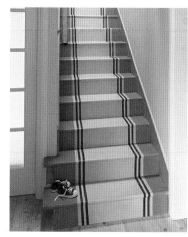

MEET THE THIS OLD HOUSE CREW

This Old House has been the leading authority on home improvement for more than three decades. Meet the TOH pros who demystify the painting process and offer time-tested advice throughout the pages of this book

Norm Abram
Master carpenter
THIS OLD HOUSE TELEVISION

As the face of the *This Old House* TV show since its premiere in 1979, and of *The New Yankee Workshop* since its debut a decade later, Norm Abram has shared his skills and insights as a carpenter and woodworker with millions of homeowners. He knows that a painted finish can do wonders to enhance woodwork, cabinetry, and furniture—and as a contributor to *This Old House* magazine, he regularly offers time-tested tips for getting the prep and brushwork just right. Norm lives with his wife, Elise, in a classic Colonial Revival that he built in Massachusetts.

Mark Powers
Senior technical editor
THIS OLD HOUSE MAGAZINE

The son of serial renovators, Mark Powers grew up helping his parents overhaul a succession of homes in the suburbs of Washington, D.C. Early in his career, he worked as an independent painting contractor and a paint store manager; he arrived at *This Old House* magazine in 2000, assuming the role of technical editor. Today he creates and manages most of the step-by-step projects that appear in the magazine's pages. Mark lives with his wife, Angelina, and their two children in a brownstone he's renovating in Brooklyn, New York.

Tom Silva
General contractor
THIS OLD HOUSE TELEVISION

For decades, Tom Silva has made the art of remodeling accessible to home enthusiasts across the country on the *This Old House* and *Ask This Old House* television shows. He knows firsthand that a paint job can only be as good as the finish work it enhances, and many have dubbed him a painter's best friend for always leaving renovated rooms with tight joints and clean surfaces. His expert advice and tricks of the trade are featured regularly in *This Old House* magazine. Tom lives with his wife, Susan, in a 19th-century house in suburban Boston that he continues to renovate.

Brian Carter

Decorative painter
CONTRIBUTOR,
THIS OLD HOUSE MAGAZINE

Brian Carter holds a bachelor's degree in interior design from Georgia State University. He is an accomplished decorative painter who has been a frequent contributor to *This Old House,* as well as many other leading national magazines, for more than a decade. In addition to running his own decorating and design business, Brian Carter Art and Design, he works as an interior stylist and produces mixed media art pieces. Brian lives with his dog, Lucky, in a 1917 Craftsman in Atlanta.

Ingrid Leess

Decorative painter
CONTRIBUTOR, THIS OLD HOUSE MAGAZINE

Ingrid Bjelland Leess is a photo stylist and self-taught designer known for her creative use of paint to transform interior spaces. Over the past 20 years, she has created hundreds of DIY features for national magazines and how-to design books, and has served as a consultant for a leading paint manufacturer. She is adept at creating sophisticated looks with simple tricks, and injecting personal flair into her designs— traits she ascribes to her Scandinavian roots. Ingrid lives in a farmhouse she renovated in New Canaan, Connecticut.

Introduction

For over 30 years—on television, online, and in print—This Old House has been the go-to resource for homeowners who are renovating, rebuilding, or creating rooms from scratch. In this guide, the first in our Weekend Remodels series, we distill our decades of experience into a one-stop workshop dedicated to the extraordinary impact of interior paint.

Here, you'll find all the tips, tools, and know-how you need to make your next paint job a success, whether your aim is to enhance the built-in beauty of a room or change its look entirely.

In step-by-step sections dedicated to areas of your home such as walls, woodwork, and floors, you'll find pro advice on how to prep, tape, and paint. Along the way we'll show you how different colors, finishes, and techniques can highlight molding and trim, make walls look like velvet, and add depth and dimension to wainscoting, bookcases, stairs, and more.

The basics are clear and concise, so you'll know what to do at every step, whether you're tackling a simple base coat or more advanced effects like faux wood grain, textured linen, or a blown-out floral. Read the how-to steps all the way through before you begin. Then get started with our top-pick tools and products—we've tested them so that you can rely on them.

As always, the goal at This Old House is to help you create a handsome, comfortable home that honors classic architectural styles but handles contemporary life with ease. And as you'll see in these first few pages, paint is an easy upgrade that Americans have been eagerly applying for centuries. To appreciate how far we've collectively come in our quest for a little color and a smoother finish, turn the page for a look at how paint has evolved over the years.

—THE EDITORS

Paint: an American history

The next time you find yourself in the paint aisle grappling over the relative merits of Celery Stalk versus Soft Sage for the guest room, try to imagine a time when each batch of paint had to be mixed by hand. The reward for all that elbow grease? The certainty that no two batches would ever turn out the same.

HOMESPUN SOLUTIONS

In early America, of course, there was no paint aisle. For the better part of the 17th century, the average colonist who wanted to perk up his place would have coated everything from walls to woodwork to ceilings in a home-brewed whitewash, which could be made by adding water to the same readily available lime used by masons to make plaster and mortar. In addition to freshening up candlelit walls, whitewash protected the plaster from wear and tear, and the caustic quality of the lime kept bugs from infesting woodwork. Lime served as both binder and pigment, but was not particularly effective in either role on the wood used extensively in New World homes.

People experimented with all sorts of other binders, including milk, tallow, alum, and salt, to improve whitewash's wear resistance and adhesion to wood. A slightly more sophisticated water-based paint option popular at the time was distemper, which used animal glue as a binder. All of these could be tinted with natural pigments, mostly iron oxides that produce earthy ochers, rusts, and browns. But they all dried into a fragile coat that would rub off if you gave it a good scrubbing. The only way to clean it up was to apply a fresh coat.

Despite the limited palette and performance of early American water-based paint, colonists found ways to decorate with color. They drew free-hand squiggle designs on woodwork, sponged dot patterns on walls, painted wood grain to mimic the look of English oak, and used stripes of lampblack

What's in paint?

The three basic ingredients have been the same for centuries: pigments, binders, and carriers.

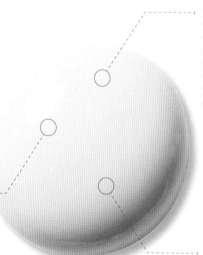

binders: Resins hold, or bind, the pigment to a surface and form a film after the carrier evaporates or oxidizes. At one time resin derived from conifer trees was dissolved in solvents to make varnish and added to oil paint to make enamel.

pigments: Powdered minerals and synthetic compounds give paint opacity and color. Colorful dirt like this Georgia earth was once used to make yellow ocher paint.

carriers: Solvents, either spirits or water, keep the binders and pigments liquefied and evenly dispersed so that they can be brushed, rolled, or sprayed.

Old recipe books

Paint historians glean insights by studying old manuals like *Directions for House and Ship Painting,* published in 1812 by one Hezekiah Reynolds.

along the bottoms of walls to create the illusion of baseboards. It was common for these dark bands to wrap all the way into fireplaces and finish with a scrolled flourish.

Many of the techniques in this book trace back to this early period, if not further. And some of them persisted until relatively recently: The practice of whitewashing, for instance, continued right up through the mid-20th century as a yearly rite of maintenance.

COLOR FOR THE COLONIES

Home decorating got a boost around 1700, when craftsmen who knew how to work with rich, durable oil paint began arriving from England—along with their secret recipe books and barrels of pricey and perishable ingredients. They would grind powdered pigments into boiled linseed oil—a hearty binder derived from flaxseed—on stone slabs, then cut the resulting paste with oil, thin it with turpentine, and apply the paint on the spot. They charged by the square yard.

By far the most important of the pigments to land on colonial shores was white lead, which had been prized in its natural form as far back as the Egyptians but whose manufacture required a laborious process that involved heating lead to its melting point of 622 degrees F as a first step. White lead provided an unrivaled opaque base that could be tinted with a huge spectrum of other pigments (save the darkest colors). It also speeded up drying time and prevented cracking.

Combined with linseed oil—which penetrates deeply, adheres tenaciously, and produces a rugged film—this made for real paint, and demand for it exploded. Because oil-based paint was much more expensive than water-based paint, it was often reserved for trim and woodwork, leaving the walls to be whitewashed or painted with a distemper solution, a practice that gave rise to the matte-meets-glossy look that persists today.

The colonial housepainter could choose from maybe three dozen pigments imported from Europe during the 18th century. Among the most exciting and sought after was Prussian blue, one of the first synthetic formulations. Invented by accident in a Berlin lab in the very early 1700s, it was a brand-new hue: a true blue that didn't tend toward violet, like indigo, yet which didn't cost a fortune, like ultramarine. Mixed with white lead, it created a medium blue that became all the rage; it cropped up in plain rural farmhouses and elite urban churches alike. When George Washington returned to Mount Vernon, he and Martha renovated with paint that included Prussian blue, no doubt relishing the fact that imported pigments, like imported tea, were no longer subject to British duties.

Mismatched In George Washington's time, paint was made in batches and consistency was iffy. Washington famously complained about color variations in the blues used at Mount Vernon, shown below.

Early pigments

Before paint came in a can, tinted with precise squirts of universal colorants, it was mixed one batch at a time with materials that came from the earth or from early chemical processes.

O ORGANIC PIGMENT

cochineal: Made from female cochineal bugs, which feed on the prickly pear cactus. Prized from Mexico to Peru before the Spanish arrived. Used mostly as a dye, it was also used to color distemper paint.

O PROCESSED PIGMENTS

red lead: Processed lead tetroxide, red lead was mixed with linseed oil to make a fast-drying primer. It was often used to paint the insides of cabinets.

chrome yellow: Crocoite, naturally occurring lead chromate, was discovered in 1770. Chemists then worked to make it artificially. The pigment went on sale around 1818 and was soon in common use.

prussian blue: The first modern artificial pigment, it was invented accidentally around 1704 by a chemist in Berlin who was trying to replicate cochineal (see above) and wound up with blue by mistake.

O EARTH-BASED PIGMENTS

burnt umber: Umber is a dull brown or greenish-brown clay when it's been dug up. It contains an iron oxide (thus its reddish tint) and a manganese oxide (the source of its brown). Umber was often painted on trim in Georgian paneled rooms or combed on doors to simulate mahogany grain.

venetian red: Venetian red was a common name for pigment derived from Italian earth rich in a ferric oxide known as hematite. It provided the barn red so popular for exteriors. The iron ore shown here came from France.

verdigris: Corroded copper is green. To make a pigment, copper sheets were exposed to vinegar fumes for weeks, yielding crystals. Verdigris darkened with age.

spanish brown: Spanish brown was made from a mixture of iron oxides that combined to create a muddier hue than that of Venetian red. It was used as a primer and as a cheap finish coat.

white lead: Lead carbonate was added to oil paints because it made them more opaque and less brittle. Relatively costly, it was made by suspending lead pieces over pots of vinegar, which were then stacked with manure or tree bark for heat and left for about two months. This produced white crystals that could be removed, broken up, and ground with oil.

terre verte: French for "green earth," terre verte was made from a variety of rocks long thought to contain copper. Now we know the color comes from an iron silicate. Somewhat drab and transparent, terre verte was mostly replaced after the mid-1800s by a mix of chrome yellow and Prussian blue.

lampblack: Lampblack is simply the soot from incompletely burned oil. Made in hooded furnaces, it was fine and somewhat greasy. It mixed well with linseed oil but not with water-based paints. Those usually called for bone black, made from animal bones burned in a closed container.

yellow ocher: Yellow ocher is the most common iron oxide. Often mixed with brown or orange, it was sold under a variety of names, including French ocher. Popular for walls and trim inside and out, it could also be tinted with white to make straw, stone, or cream colors.

Decorative art
Stenciling was an inexpensive alternative to wallpaper in the late 18th and early 19th centuries. The room shown at left, in Old Sturbridge Village, Massachusetts, is a classic example.

A REVOLUTIONARY INDUSTRY

As America tottered into its new independence, it sought to build up its own industries to avoid importing goods from Britain. The first American factory to produce white lead was established in Philadelphia in 1804, and that led to the sale of a paste containing white lead and linseed oil—a major step toward standardizing paint.

Farmers began growing more flax, and the commercial preparation of pigments expanded color choice. When chrome yellow appeared in 1818, it opened the way to a slew of new greens. The passion for painting grew right along with the country's middle class, which went for elaborate, bright color schemes meant to imitate the mansions of the upper class. Companies would mix batches of popular colors every spring, and people would hurry home with containers of it, hoping to use it before it separated. But these were poor, adulterated mixtures.

It wasn't until after the Civil War that the first high-quality factory-made paints arrived. They came courtesy of one Henry Sherwin, who teamed up with two partners to launch Sherwin-Williams & Company. He devised a new way to pulverize pigments for even dispersal and, crucially, patented a handy resealable can, which allowed paint to be packaged, shipped, and used anywhere. At long last the average American could buy a can of paint with reasonable expectations for what was inside and how it would go on.

MAKING A STATEMENT

Once good paint was readily available, color trends took off. The Victorians couldn't get enough. They slapped on vibrant shades of purple and red to feed their fascination with exotic foreign goods and to highlight intricate plasterwork. In a backlash to all that color, Arts and Crafts homes featured more subdued tones and even unpainted wood trim. During the Art Deco period that followed, rich colors like crimson were used alongside metallic finishes to enliven crisp white-and-black motifs. The 1940s brought subdued ivories and grays, and then every decade thereafter seemed to develop its own signature palette.

By the time the Avocado 1970s arrived, oil paint was losing out to water-soluble formulations enabled by the introduction of remarkable plastic resins, which provided good durability and adhesion yet allowed cleanup with a wet sponge. Generally known as latex paints, these caught on quickly. Toward the end of the decade, titanium dioxide replaced white lead, which had been proved to be a health hazard.

Chemists are still hard at it today, trying to remove the last solvents containing volatile organic compounds (VOCs) from paint. At the same time, digital technology and other advances make it possible to re-create any color and mix it consistently from can to can. New speciality paints are available for every surface and design.

Unlike the balky concoctions of centuries past, paint is now a problem solver, the easiest way to transform a room. That's because today's formulations go on so nicely that your biggest concern truly is settling on that perfect shade of green.

CHAPTER 1

Getting started

A can of paint is so full of promise. It holds the potential to clean-sweep dingy walls and brighten your outlook. Luckily, today's quality paints and tools make quick work of freshening up your rooms. But before you pick up a brush, you should consider the function of the space: Is it a high-traffic or high-humidity area? Do you want to encourage conviviality or rest and relaxation? How you'll use the room, and what effect you want to create, are key to choosing a paint formulation, sheen, and color. Coming up: the basics you need to begin your paint transformation.

Paint

○ TYPES OF PAINT

Think about style and about function. Paint comes in a range of finishes, from light-reflecting to utterly flat, and can perform a number of tricks

Primer: A coat of primer lays the foundation for a lasting paint job. Primers are formulated with special binders that help them adhere to a surface and provide a grippy base for the top coat. Consider asking your paint store to tint the primer to match your paint to ensure even color coverage.

Latex: Water-soluble latex is DIY-friendly because it cleans up with soap and water. Most paint today is vinyl acrylic or 100 percent acrylic latex. In some states, it's the only option in gallons as more limits are put on the sale of oil-based products. Latex paint dries quickly, usually in two hours, and "cures" in a matter of weeks.

Glaze: Semitranslucent resin-rich glazes can be tinted with paint or concentrated colorants to create special effects. With the help of brushes, rollers, sponges, or other specialty tools, glazes can be used to mimic textured fabrics or vintage plaster. Because glaze dries slowly, it allows you to blend and rework patterns until you're happy with the results.

Oil: Also known as solvent-based or alkyd paint, it dries slowly and must be cleaned up with mineral spirits. But that slow drying time helps oil paint level out, reducing visible brush strokes and roller marks. Oil paint also hardens well to create a durable finish.

Where to use which finish

Choose the right sheen for the job, whether it's highlighting living room trim, masking dings in the foyer, or making sure your kitchen walls are easy to clean. Flat low-luster paints roughen the surface to create an even coat that hides flaws. Glossier paints form a smoother, more wear-resistant finish—but they can also highlight imperfections. Though the choice ultimately comes down to personal preference, here are some guidelines to consider.

Gloss
> *good for trim, doors, cabinets*

Glossy finishes can stand up to assaults that would ruin a flat finish, and they clean well. For the toughest finish of all, go for a glossy oil paint. Paint: Pratt & Lambert's Designer White (wainscot)

Semigloss
> *good for baths, kitchens, trim*

The finish of choice for rooms devoted to bathing and cooking, semigloss is less shiny than gloss and almost as easy to clean. In a bath, choose one with mildewcide. Paint: Glidden's Windswept (walls) and White on White (wainscot)

Satin, Eggshell
> *good for foyers, high-traffic areas, family spaces*

These warm, reflective finishes have less sheen than semigloss. They also clean more easily than a matte or flat, and resist "burnishing," the shiny spots that develop when rubbed or scrubbed. Paint: C2 Paint's Temptation (walls)

Matte
> *good for bedrooms, living rooms, dining rooms*

These low-gloss finishes deliver a deep, rich coat of color. They're a popular choice for living spaces, where they can help camouflage tiny cracks and bumps. Paint: Glidden's Cactus Dahlia

Flat
> *good for ceilings, living areas*

Flat finishes have little or no shine, so they create an even tone and hide surface imperfections. But they can be harder to clean than finishes with a little more sheen. There are even extra-flats made specifically for ceilings. Paint: Valspar's Clean White

Low-VOC

Paint ingredients contain volatile organic compounds (VOCs) that off-gas, creating that familiar paint smell and a potential hazard to your health. Paint companies are working overtime to reduce or remove these compounds without sacrificing good color and even coverage. Today there are many low-VOC lines on the market and more and more no-VOC offerings.

○ SPECIALTY PAINTS

Get the look you want—and the performance you need—with formulations that deliver something special. Here are a few to consider

Magnetic paint
When the front of the fridge runs out of space for photos and drawings, create a new place to hang them with this iron-infused paint. It's generally sold as a primer, so two or more coats (plus any top coat color you desire) can turn a wall, door, or framed piece of wood into a message center or display space. Paint: Rust-Oleum's Magnetic Latex Primer under Behr's Farmhouse Red

Milk paint In early America, paint was sometimes made on the spot with milk, lime, and natural pigments. Today, milk paint is an easy way to give walls and furniture a vintage look, and it comes in dozens of colors. Whip it up in no time using a kitchen hand mixer or blender and a just-add-water powder. Designed to give walls a more even tone than milk paints of yore, these new formulations can go right over drywall. Paint: SafePaint's Tavern Green

Stainless steel
This specialty paint can add a sleek, modern accent to any room. Sure, you could use it to update your fridge, but it can also give a new look to furniture, picture frames, tables, or even a junk-store lamp. Paint: Thomas' Liquid Stainless Steel

Chalkboard paint It's easy to create a giant erasable calendar, foot-long memo pad, or even canister labels with latex paint that acts like chalkboard. Choose traditional schoolhouse gray and mix in some white to get various tints. Or go for one of a host of new colors, including turquoise.
Paint: Hudson Paint's So Stone

{ Tools }

○ BRUSHES & APPLICATORS

A painter's primary helper, a good brush holds and releases paint more controllably than a cheap one. Treat it right, and your investment will last for years

Natural-bristle brushes
Made with hairs snipped from the hides of Chinese hogs, these brushes work best with oil paint. Their naturally flagged tips hold paint in the edges and release it throughout the stroke instead of all at once on first contact. Natural bristles absorb too much moisture to be used effectively with water-based latex.

Synthetic brushes
A brush of nylon and polyester filaments applies latex paint exceptionally well. The bristles should be "flagged": tapered, split, and arranged in multiple lengths to form a slim, chiseled tip. You'll want at least one 2½-inch angled sash brush for cutting in along trim and painting woodwork, and one 3-inch straight brush for cutting in along walls and ceilings and painting large panels.

[TIP]
HOW TO HOLD A BRUSH
Painting is easy, but the repetitive movements can leave you feeling achy if you don't hold the tools correctly. Gently pinch the base of the brush between your index finger and thumb along the bottom of the metal ferrule. It's much like holding a pencil.

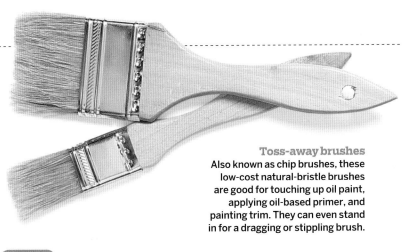

Artist's brushes
Good for touch-ups and delicate freehand painting, these brushes come in a variety of shapes and sizes.

Toss-away brushes
Also known as chip brushes, these low-cost natural-bristle brushes are good for touching up oil paint, applying oil-based primer, and painting trim. They can even stand in for a dragging or stippling brush.

pro advice NORM ABRAM, TOH MASTER CARPENTER

PAINTBRUSH PREP

"Before you start painting, soak your brush in the liquid you'll ultimately use to clean it—water for latex paint, mineral spirits for oil. Then place the handle between your palms and rub them together to spin the brush dry. This helps the paint release from the bristles more smoothly. Plus it makes cleanup at the end of the day a lot easier."

Disposable foam brushes
They come in many widths and are great for small jobs or touch-ups because they are pliable and can fit into crevices. They apply paint very smoothly and don't spatter.

What to look for in a brush

The ultimate test of a brush's quality is how well it picks up and releases paint. Unfortunately, you can't check that in the hardware-store aisle, but here are some other things you can look for.

A chiseled tip Look at the brush in profile. The bristles should come to a tapered point—this gives you more control because they form a narrow line as you press the brush against the work surface.

Soft bristles Touch the tips to your cheek or the back of your hand. Cheap brushes feel stiff and coarse; feathery, soft ones will apply paint smoothly.

Full body The cardboard or wood spacer creates a void that on good brushes holds a reservoir of paint. On cheap brushes, thick spacers make up for a deficit of bristles. Pinch the bristles between your fingers near their base. If they feel thin, you'll be dipping that brush a lot.

Firm construction Tug on the bristles. If they come out in your hand, they'll come out on whatever you're painting. The ferrule, the metal band that helps hold the bristles in place, should be nailed through the handle and made of rust-resistant stainless or plated steel, or copper.

Price A quality brush, one made by hand, runs $10 and up.

Stencil brushes
These stiff, flattop brushes are used for "pouncing" paint onto a surface.

Wood-graining rocker
This ingenious tool applies a realistic wood-grain finish complete with knots to any surface when pulled and rocked through paint or glaze.

Dragging brush
As the name suggests, you drag this natural-bristle brush through glaze to create a lined pattern, often called strié.

Steel wool
Loosened and pulled apart, steel wool becomes a good tool for creating a fine linen effect when pulled through glaze. Beware of leaving filings behind in latex paint—they'll rust.

Stippling brush
This densely bristled brush creates a finely dotted pattern when pounced on a wall covered in glaze.

Rags
For cleanup they are essential—most latex errors wipe off easily with a damp rag—but cotton rags are also great applicators for paint or glaze. Scrunched or rolled, they can be used to create interesting textures.

super-saver
Here's an easy way to make your own stippling brush. Gang together five or six chip brushes. Bind them at the ferrules and handles with tape.

pro advice TOM SILVA, TOH GENERAL CONTRACTOR
TEMPORARY STORAGE
"When a painting job lasts more than a day, scrape excess paint off your brush and roller, and seal them in a plastic zipper bag. Press out as much air as you can so that the paint doesn't dry. Then pop the bag in the refrigerator. It'll keep for up to a week."

Comb
A flexible rubber three-sided comb allows you to create intricate ridged designs when pulled through paint or glaze. Each side offers a different pattern.

Spatter brush
Made with stiff synthetic bristles, this brush sprays a random pattern of paint droplets when tapped.

Sponge
Use a natural sea sponge to overlay a top coat color and create a softly mottled effect. You can also cut divots into a synthetic sponge to achieve a similar look.

How to clean your brush

A good brush deserves to be cleaned well and often. When cleaning brushes used with oil paint, wear rubber gloves to protect your hands, and work in a well-ventilated area to prevent solvent fumes from accumulating.

1_ Thin. For latex paint, vigorously force water mixed with dish soap into the bristles, then tip the brush up so that it seeps down into the ferrule. When cleaning brushes used in oil paint, use mineral spirits, following the same cleaning process.

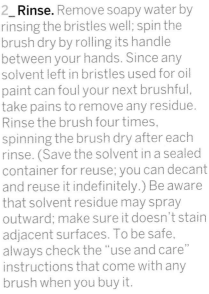

2_ Rinse. Remove soapy water by rinsing the bristles well; spin the brush dry by rolling its handle between your hands. Since any solvent left in bristles used for oil paint can foul your next brushful, take pains to remove any residue. Rinse the brush four times, spinning the brush dry after each rinse. (Save the solvent in a sealed container for reuse; you can decant and reuse it indefinitely.) Be aware that solvent residue may spray outward; make sure it doesn't stain adjacent surfaces. To be safe, always check the "use and care" instructions that come with any brush when you buy it.

3_ Brush. After spinning the brush for the last time, straighten the bristles and banish any remaining paint particles with a small metal-bristle brush or paintbrush comb.

4_ Wrap. Unless you protect the cleaned bristles, they'll collect dust and lose their shape before their next use. Wrap the bristles in a stiff paper sleeve—like the one that originally came with the brush—so that they stay clean and straight. Store the brush flat or hang it up by the hole in its handle.

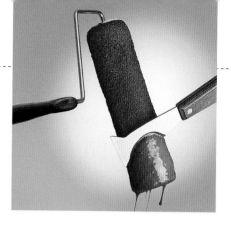

○ROLLERS & PADS

Nothing is faster than a roller or a pad for getting paint out of the tray and onto the wall. Made from absorbent fabric or foam, they hold more liquid than brushes and distribute it more evenly

How to clean your roller

Place the roller on the edge of a bucket. Using a curved scraper (like the one on a painter's 5-in-1 tool), push excess paint off the roller cover into the bucket. Turn the roller each time you scrape, as if you're peeling a carrot. Wash off remaining paint with water (for latex) or solvent (for oil).

Roller frames
Quality frames hold covers tight and minimize flex. Small rollers are handy for painting door panels or wainscot. Look for reinforced threaded handles that'll stand up to painting with a pole.

Pad
With guide wheels and an extension pole socket, small pads can put paint on a flat-paneled door or cut in around a room more quickly and neatly than a brush. And unlike rollers, they don't spatter.

smooth
⅛- to ¼-inch nap cover for very smooth surfaces (plaster, laminate, metal)

semismooth
⅜- to ½- inch nap cover for lightly textured walls (drywall, wood)

rough
¾-inch nap cover for textured walls (stucco, brick)

Choosing roller covers

Roller covers come in a variety of materials, pile lengths (naps), and sizes. As a rule, avoid the cheapest; their cardboard cores break down and they shed fibers.

When picking a cover, match the fibers to the paint type. Polyester or nylon covers are ideal for water-based paint. Natural-fiber covers, made of mohair or lamb's wool, are best for oil paint. Foam covers work with all paints, but they're best on mini rollers. This setup is ideal for getting a lot of paint onto porous surfaces, such as wood paneling or cabinets, and for creating supersmooth finishes with glossier paints. Look for firm, high-density foam; squishy, inexpensive foam won't stand up to rolling pressure and may cause drips.

○PAINTING GEAR

Here's your checklist of must-have items for a successful paint job

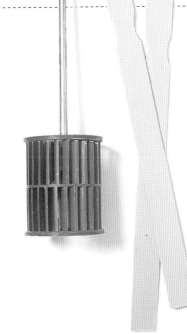

Stir sticks
Paint stores hand these out for a reason: Paint naturally separates. Exert a little muscle with the traditional wood stirrer or use a paddle attachment with your drill/driver.

Cut bucket with liner
Never dip your paintbrush directly into the can—too sloppy, too risky if the container slips or drips, and too likely to contaminate the paint with surface debris. For optimum control, pour paint into a small metal cut bucket fitted with a liner and fill it only one-third of the way. Paint cups with liners are good for small paint jobs.

Extension pole
Longer reach means fewer trips up and down the ladder when painting walls or ceilings. A two-handed grip is also easier on arms, neck, and shoulders. A telescoping pole is useful for lofty spaces. Place your hands 18 inches apart for best roller control.

Roller pan and liner
Invest in a rigid metal pan that won't bend when you pick it up. Look for liners that are a good fit and have lots of grate marks.

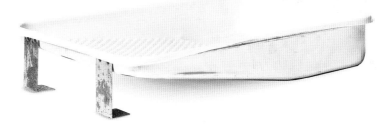

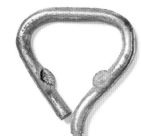

Paint-can key
Give your screwdriver a rest and open lids with the tool designed for the task. The key won't bend the lid's lip, so the can will reseal more easily.

Spout
An inexpensive plastic snap-on spout makes pouring paint into a roller pan or cut bucket much easier and keeps the lid rim from becoming clogged with paint.

Ladder
Choose a step ladder with a sturdy tray. Some come with molded cradles for your cut bucket and hooks for your rags.

pro advice
TOM SILVA, TOH GENERAL CONTRACTOR
LADDER SAFETY
"Stand on a low rung, with your body centered between the ladder rails and both feet firmly planted. Use the ladder tray to hold your pail so that you can keep one hand free. Never stand on one of the top two rungs or overreach; both can throw you off balance."

○PREP TOOLS

Preparing surfaces before you paint is time-consuming, sure, but it's also crucial. Here are the essentials you'll need for a smooth, even finish and to protect other surfaces in the room

Window scraper and razor blades
Standard razor blades remove errant paint strokes from glass. A spritz of water first prevents scratching. Or try a plastic blade—it won't scratch.

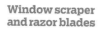

Tape
These painter's tapes protect surfaces while giving you crisp edges to paint along and cut in on. For designs that call for stripes or other straight lines along the wall, use one infused with polymers that will create a gel barrier to fight seeping when paint touches the tape. Shown: FrogTape Multi-Surface [1]. For general masking, use a UV-resistant tape that is rated for 14 days of adhesion time. Shown: ScotchBlue Painter's Tape [2]. And for projects that you know you'll be spreading out over a few weekends, look for a long-lasting tape that can be safely kept in place for up to 60 days. Shown: ShurRelease CP 60 [3].

Drop cloths
Disposable 4-mil plastic drop cloths over rosin paper or newspaper will work but can be slippery. If you plan to do much painting, buy canvas—it's reusable and absorbs drips that puddle on plastic. Plastic is still handy for protecting furniture and fixtures, though.

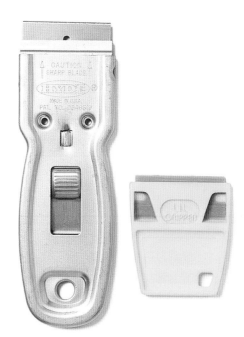

pro advice
MARK POWERS,
TOH SENIOR TECHNICAL EDITOR

CAULKING TIPS
"Pull, rather than push, the caulk gun in a smooth motion as you squeeze its trigger. Control the flow of caulk by adjusting the speed at which you pull the tip along."

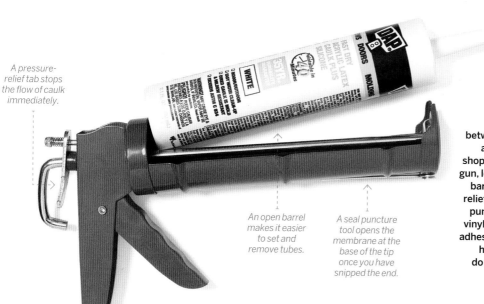

A pressure-relief tab stops the flow of caulk immediately.

Caulk and caulk gun
Caulk any gaps between woodwork and walls. When shopping for a caulk gun, look for an open barrel, a pressure-relief tab, and a seal puncture tool. Use vinyl or latex acrylic adhesive caulk. Both have good body, do not shrink, and are paintable.

An open barrel makes it easier to set and remove tubes.

A seal puncture tool opens the membrane at the base of the tip once you have snipped the end.

[TIP]

WHICH GRIT TO PICK?

Use a medium grit (100 or 120) when you're prepping walls that are already in decent shape, and a coarser grit (60 or 80) to take the edges off paint that is chipped or peeled. Very-fine grit (200 or 220) is best for smoothing surfaces between coats of paint.

Sandpaper

Look for black sandpaper coated with silicon carbide—it won't gunk up as quickly as standard-issue aluminium oxide papers, so it'll last longer. Foam sanding sponges covered with the same stuff allow you to sneak into corners and evenly wrap around curved trim—plus they're reusable. Just wring them out in water to clean them. You can even use them damp to trap dust while sanding.

Putty knife and fillers

For a smooth finish you need to address holes, dents, and scratches first. Use lightweight spackling on walls. Premixed and setting-type joint compounds are best for skimming and filling large areas. On trim, try either water putty or a two-part wood filler.

Sanding head and pole

A pole sander puts ceilings and the tops of walls within reach without a ladder. Later, you can attach the pole to your roller frame for painting walls and ceilings.

The 5-in-1 tool

a must-have

Like the subject of a late-night infomercial, the 5-in-1 painter's multitool has a pitch that's hard to resist: Get a putty knife, roller cleaner, hammer, scraper, and spreader—all on one easy-to-wield handle! Whichever brand you choose, make sure your multitool has a stiff steel blade about 2 to 3 inches wide, with smooth, burr-free edges. Wiggle the blade and the little metal end cap to make sure both are firmly fastened. You'll be putting some pressure on the handle when scraping, so avoid one made of cheap plastic; instead, choose a grip made of wood or nonslip rubber.

Open lids. The wide tip fits beneath the lip of a paint-can lid, and a simple twist pops it off without marring it. Do the same to loosen a piece of molding, or run it along a strip of painter's tape to tuck it into a corner.

Rake joints. The sharp point cleans out cracks in plaster, digs out old caulk, and cuts through paint layers between window sashes.

Clean rollers. This half-round cutout helps remove paint from roller covers.

Scrape. The straight, beveled edge scrapes peeling paint or wallpaper.

Pull nails. The teardrop-shaped opening will pull a nail, but be careful—the action can cause the scraper blade to damage a finished surface. Also use it to lever the cap off a tube of glue or pop a plug of dried caulk from a nozzle.

Spread. Like a putty knife, it spreads and smooths wood filler or spackling. Models with stiff steel blades can unstick painted-over switch plates.

Pound nails. The metal end cap can hammer protruding nails or tap down a loose lid. Striking it gently with a mallet transforms the tool into a chisel for cutting through thick layers of old paint.

{ Color }

People are aware that they respond positively to color—that it can soothe them, delight them, inspire them—but often they're so afraid of making a mistake that they retreat to the safety of white. If you're not sure how to select colors you'll feel comfortable with, here are some surefire pointers.

IDENTIFY THE COLORS YOU LIKE

The first step is to take stock of the colors that already resonate with you. Look in your closet: You've spent a lifetime honing your color preferences through the clothes you wear, so look beyond the black and gray business suits to colors in sweaters, neckties, scarves, and shirts that you instinctively gravitate toward.

Another helpful step is to tear out pictures from magazines and mark pages in books that show rooms painted in colors you like. Once you've assembled a folderful, go back and really look through them to see what mood emerges. Then pay attention to the colors you selected most consistently.

You can also take color cues from fabric, a rug, or a piece of art that you plan to use in the room you're painting. (Often it works best to choose a subtler accent color, instead of the dominant color in the pattern, to play up the walls.) Not only will these sources help you coordinate colors within this area of your home, but you're also undoubtedly drawing on furnishings you've picked over time because you're comfortable with them.

CONSIDER THE WHOLE ROOM

Colors don't exist in isolation. So once you've narrowed your color preferences and picked up paint chips for the project at hand, your next step is to put those chips together with the other elements in the room: furniture, floor coverings, window treatments. See how they affect the colors you're considering.

The easiest way to do this is to create a color idea board with fabric swatches and floor finishes, or, when you don't have actual samples, the approximate colors of every element in the room and adjacent spaces. As you sift through your paint chips, view them along with all the components on the board. Treating the space as a whole creates a more cohesive look, which will make your home feel more expansive.

Avoid paint-chip overload

The rows and rows of paint choices at your local home center can be overwhelming. Bringing a reference from the room you're painting—a slipcover or a piece of pottery—can make the process of selecting colors go faster.

Find colors you love
Color inspiration is everywhere in your house—rugs, upholstery, ceramics, beads, ribbon, antiques, neckties, fabric; virtually anything can spark a color palette.

○COLOR 101

The color wheel, which shows how colors relate to one another, is a useful tool for selecting colors in combination. Here are some of the terms designers and color pros use to describe color, which will help you in talking—and thinking—about it

Primary colors are the basic ones—red, blue, and yellow—from which all other colors are made.

Secondary colors are made by mixing two primary colors.

Tertiary colors are made by mixing a primary color and a secondary color.

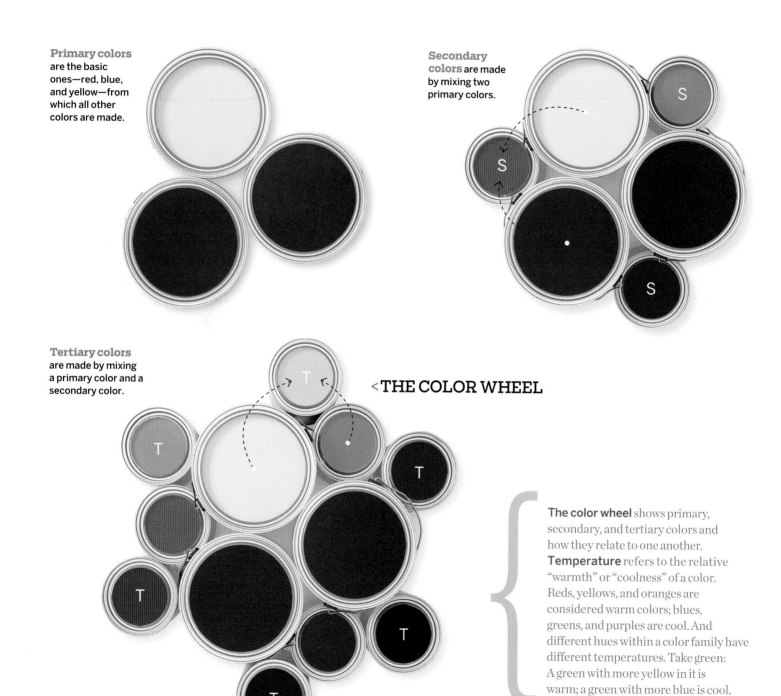

< **THE COLOR WHEEL**

The color wheel shows primary, secondary, and tertiary colors and how they relate to one another. **Temperature** refers to the relative "warmth" or "coolness" of a color. Reds, yellows, and oranges are considered warm colors; blues, greens, and purples are cool. And different hues within a color family have different temperatures. Take green: A green with more yellow in it is warm; a green with more blue is cool.

Analogous colors are neighboring colors on the wheel, such as yellow, yellow-orange, and orange. Using them together generally creates a harmonious effect.

Tint is a color mixed with white.

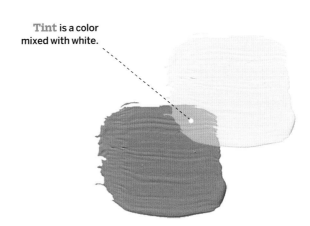

Complementary colors are opposites on the color wheel—red and green, yellow and violet, and blue and orange. Used together, they enhance and intensify each other's energy.

Shade is a color mixed with black.

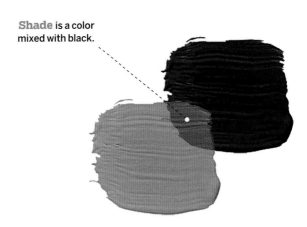

Monochromatic colors are tints, shades, and tones of the same color, such as lavender, plum, and violet. Together they create a subtle, restful feeling.

Tone is a color mixed with gray.

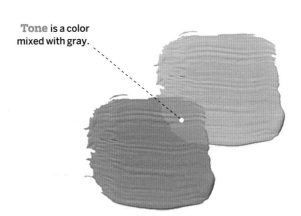

WHAT COLOR WHERE

While we all have our own individual reactions to color, every hue also has general visual and psychological effects that can influence how we experience it. It's important to take those properties into consideration before you paint a room, to ensure that the color suits the room's purpose

Red is intense and high energy. It represents passion. Said to stimulate both appetite and conversation, it's a favorite choice for dining rooms. Red also spices up small spaces, such as foyers and libraries.

Statement maker
Red walls and a red ceiling make this large dining room more intimate while highlighting the white wainscot and trim. Red overhead lowers the ceiling visually, making the space feel cozier and more convivial—a plus in a room designed for conversation. Paint: C2 Paint's Red Stiletto and Sheer (moldings)

Monochromatic approach
Wrap a room in a single color for an elegant look. Using the same paint for wall paneling, doors, and moldings, such as the fiery tomato gloss used here, adds drama to this den. Paint: Ace Paint's Flamenco

Warmed-up walls
Red doesn't have to feel heavy. A single bright wall in this dining area works because the surrounding palette is neutral. It gives the room a modern feel. Paint: Olympic's Sunset Skyline

Pink,
a softer form of red, creates a flattering glow and can offer a sense of security.

Dip-dyed effect
A faux wainscot created with a darker shade of pink suggests an architectural element in a simple bedroom. Paint: Benjamin Moore's Strawberry Yogurt (above) and Damask Rose (below)

Orange is warm and lively and lends a cheerful mood to a room. Subtler tints, such as apricot and peach, are flattering to everyone; they also harmonize with a lot of other colors. Deep orange hues, like terra-cotta, have a warmth that works especially well on textured or faux-painted surfaces.

Dramatic lines
Rich terra-cotta-colored walls highlight the interesting ceiling angles and Gothic arched window in this bedroom. Paint: Ralph Lauren Paint's Villa Torlonia

Warm glow
Burnished orange walls in this front foyer harmonize with the various wood tones in the space. Paint: Pratt & Lambert's Acorn

Inspiring bright
A yellow-orange wall flanking the window amplifies this room's natural light. Set up as a workstation, the room benefits from the hue's uplifting energy. Paint: Sherwin-Williams' Sunrise

Vivid contrast Khaki-yellow walls and golden-olive trim create a color-saturated backdrop for rich blue cabinets. C2 Paint's Sisal (walls) and Cheetah (shelves, trim), and Pratt & Lambert's Indigo (cabinets)

Yellow, the brightest of the colors, is sunny and vibrant. It stimulates creativity, makes people happy, and increases attentiveness. Yellow helps brighten a north-facing room and is a natural choice for kitchens and other rooms where you spend the early part of the day.

Pure gold
Soft flaxen walls, with a green undertone picked up in the accessories, help ground an airy, light-filled sitting area. Paint: Valspar's Fall Meadow

Color drenched
Yellow walls with green wainscot help set off this dining area while red accents and a turquoise-and-black table tie it in to the kitchen. Paint: Behr's Mellow Yellow (walls), Japanese Fern (wainscot), Black Suede (trim), Grenadine (switch plates), and Botanical Tint (door)

Green, which represents nature and renewal, is soothing. Because it's a balance of warm (yellow) and cool (blue), it's versatile and easy to live with. Dark green, associated with money and prestige, is also thought to promote concentration. As a result, it's a popular choice for studies and libraries. Fresh apple greens or soft sage greens are a good way to update traditional interiors.

Garden party Grass-green walls set a rich tone in a formal space. Paint: Behr's Thyme Green

Fun and colorful Three electric green walls and a fourth tiled in bright blue energize a laundry room. Dark slate tiles on the floor are a practical choice and temper all that bright color. Paint: Behr's Key Lime

Soothing canvas Blue-green walls and ceiling are a pleasant backdrop for the real star of the room: the massive exposed beams and decorative Gothic trusses. Paint: Sherwin-Williams' Restful

Blue is tranquil and calming. Its cool tones promote relaxation, making it ideal for bedrooms and baths. Blue's comforting familiarity is also associated with honesty and integrity. Pale or soft gray-blues are easiest to use on walls, but brighter cobalt blues can work well as accents.

Perked-up panels
Vibrant blue milk paint highlights the cozy slope of the ceiling in this upstairs bedroom. Paint: The Old Fashioned Milk Paint Co.'s 75 percent White, 20 percent Federal Blue, and 5 percent Light Cream

Neutral territory
Gray-blue walls lend a sophisticated look to a country interior. Paint: Benjamin Moore's Misty Memories

Soothing sanctuary
Ice-blue walls and warm white trim make this attic bath feel fresh and inviting. Benjamin Moore's Sapphireberry (walls) and White Dove (trim)

Purple stimulates creativity and is associated with royalty. It's generally too intense to use for anything more than accents, though a deep eggplant is effective in a small space. Paler shades, like lavender and lilac, can be restful and soothing.

Cool tones
A palette of silver, gray, and white gives a sophisticated edge to a dining area wrapped in lilac. Paint: Ralph Lauren Paint's Spring Violet

Deep and dark
Charcoal-purple walls and ebonized floors create a dramatic backdrop for a mix of traditional and modern furnishings. Paint: C2 Paint's Scooter (walls) and Essence (trim)

Shifting away from neutral
A monochromatic scheme of flax, beige, and blond-wood tones gets a refreshing style boost from lavender walls. Paint: Olympic's Lilac Time

White represents cleanliness, neutrality, and purity (why else would brides wear it?). It can help us clear our minds and start anew.

Attic aerie
Enhance a small space by coating every surface in white. The absence of color opens up low-ceiling areas, making them feel airier. Paint: Benjamin Moore's Navajo White

Milk and cream
A palette of soft whites makes a cottage-style bath feel serene. An abundance of light through the French doors and skylight ensures that the creamy white paint will look rich instead of dingy. Paint: Valspar's Frosted Shadow

How to choose the right white

People who get confounded by paint colors often default to white. But there are so many variations of the hue that the choice can still be bewildering. The first thing to consider is that most whites are either "warm" or "cool." To figure out which is right for your space, test a few shades to see how they work with the other colors at play in the room.

Warm whites incorporate an undertone of yellow—think French-vanilla ice cream—or a touch of rust, pink, or brown. Warm colors appear to advance, so a creamy white can make a large space seem cozier.

Cool whites have green, blue, or gray undertones. Crisp and clean-looking, they lend themselves well to modern spaces. Because cool colors appear to recede, a cool white can visually expand a small room.

Pure whites are the whitest of whites, formulated with few or no tinted undertones. So-called clean whites are most often used on ceilings, to create a neutral field above and visually lift the ceiling height.

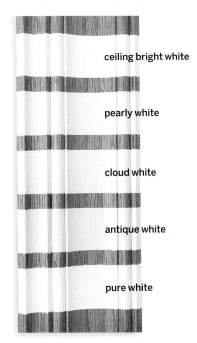

ceiling bright white

pearly white

cloud white

antique white

pure white

TIPS FOR USING COLOR

Here, 27 inspiring ideas for transforming your home with bucket, brush, and roller—plus five mistakes to avoid

PICKING COLORS

1_ Expect the paint to be more intense than the chip. The color will generally look more saturated when applied to the walls of a room, so if you're unsure, you may want to go a notch higher on the paint chip strip and select a paler version.

2_ Use warm colors to draw in walls or ceiling. Similarly, use cool colors to make them recede. A room painted a warm color will feel more intimate, while a cool color can make a room feel more expansive.

3_ Consider what feeling and effect you want to create. If your goal is to make the room appear larger, go with lighter shades. But if you want to accentuate its coziness, opt for rich, saturated hues. Then think about the room's function. Sunny colors often work well in the breakfast nook where you enjoy your morning coffee, while calming shades in a bathroom can encourage you to de-stress in the tub after a demanding day.

4_ Try layering before repainting. If you don't like a color once it's on the walls, here's a trick: Apply a glaze or color wash in a darker or lighter shade to shift the color and give it more depth and luminosity.

Paint: C2 Paint's Bonanza (walls) and Cheetah (trim)

5

Save stronger or bolder colors for rooms you pass through or spend less time in, such as an entry, a formal dining room, or a powder room.

COLOR COMBOS

6_ Adopt the 60-30-10 rule to balance multiple colors. Use a dominant color for 60 percent of the room, a recessive one for 30 percent, and an accent color for 10 percent.

7_ Try this foolproof recipe for combining colors: Pick shades from the same paint chip strip.

8_ Use color to define an area in an open plan. It can delineate space for a specific activity.

9

Unify your living spaces. Wall colors that relate to each other draw the eye from one area to the next, creating a harmonious flow.

Paint: Valspar's Field of Pines (near wall) and Heart of Palm (far wall)

What's the most reliable way to test a paint color?

Even the pros test a color, often several colors, in the actual setting before choosing one. Paint a swath on the wall at least 5 or 6 feet wide from floor to ceiling, applying two coats. A quart of paint runs about $12, but many companies offer smaller, tester sizes. Don't get less than a pint, though—you won't have enough for an effective test patch.

In the test area, rehang the art and put the furniture back in place. Take a few days to live with the color to see how the light and furnishings in the room affect it. Check out how it looks both day and night.

Painting on foam board or posterboard is another option, and it allows you to move the color around the room to see how it looks in different lights—by the window, say, or in a corner, or next to the sofa.

10

Find successful bold pairings across from each other on the color wheel.

Paint: (clockwise from top left) Sherwin-Williams' Festival Green (paneling) and Venture Violet (wall); Pratt & Lambert's Osprey (wall) and Rye (wainscot); Benjamin Moore's Rust (near walls) and Sandalwood (far walls); Valspar's Pale Butter (wall) and La Fonda Deep Blue (French doors)

11

Brighten built-ins. A hit of color can turn the functional elements in a room into eye-catching focal points.

Paint: Olympic's Golden Glow (built-in)

12_ Be bold and try using two different colors in the same room. For instance, paint a built-in bookcase or a niche a shade of green in a room with blue walls, which will highlight the items on the bookcase or inside the recessed area.

13_ Don't be bashful in the kitchen. An activity-oriented gathering space, the kitchen is ideal for energetic color, a lively departure from traditional white.

19

Use an accent wall to set off a room's best assets. A single field of color can highlight the built-in details, and the artwork and furnishings you introduce.

NEUTRALS

14_ Know that *neutral* doesn't have to mean "boring."
There are many neutrals with attitude, and they are far more interesting than basic white or beige. Take a look at dark taupe, paper-bag brown, dark khaki, sage, gray-greens, and muted yellows.

15_ Put the focus on a dominant color. Surround it with neutrals.

CREATE AN ILLUSION

16_ Hide flaws. If you want to downplay elements in a room—the windows that are off-center, say, or the radiator you can't move—make them disappear by painting them the same color as the walls.

17_ Make a room feel bigger.
A lot of contrast can make a room seem small. To make a space feel larger, use similar pale tones on all the surfaces.

18_ Or make it feel smaller and cozier. If you're aiming to create a welcoming atmosphere in a foyer, study, or library, for example, hunter green or rust may serve you better than pale peach or celery.

Paint: Glidden's Dress Blues (accent wall) and Ruffled Feathers (other walls)

20

Try an unexpected pairing of a pastel and a neutral to give a room a fresh look.

Paint: Benjamin Moore's Rock Harbor Violet (above) and Waynesboro Taupe (below)

Five common color mistakes to avoid

> **Being afraid.** The best way to get over color fear is to start with a hue you love—like one from a rug, a painting, or a fabric. Then test it on the wall. If it's too strong, ask your paint store to mix it at "half strength" by lightening it with white or to tone it down by adding more gray.

> **Putting too much on the walls.** Be aware of the intensity of the colors in a room. If you have a rug with five or six strong colors, don't paint the walls in equally strong hues. Let the rug be the focal point and the walls a lighter color.

> **Putting too little on the walls.** If you think your room is boring, look at it in terms of the 60-30-10 rule that designers often employ: 60 percent of the color in a space generally comes from the walls; 30 percent from upholstery, floor coverings, or window treatments; and 10 percent from accent pieces, accessories, and artwork. Translation: Liven up those white walls.

> **Rushing the process.** The best way to find colors you can live with is to keep on testing: Paint a large swath on the wall and live with it for a day or two so that you can see it in both natural and artificial light.

> **Forgetting about primer.** When changing the color of a wall, primer (white or tinted) is vital to getting the actual color you picked out. It ensures there will be no interference from the previous color.

26

When you're pairing two bold colors, using crisp white trim between them lets the colors shine singly and as a pair.

CEILINGS

21_ Give low ceilings the illusion of height. Paint them white, and any crown molding the same color as the wall; the result will keep your upward gaze from being interrupted.

22_ Don't be afraid to break the rules. Generally, ceilings are best left white, but a touch of color can warm things up and give a space a more finished look. Just keep in mind that warm shades lose their yellow tones on surfaces where no sunlight ever falls, turning bluer and grayer, aka dingy.

HANDLING TRIM

23_ Reverse the conventional scheme. Trim doesn't have to be light. Paint moldings a slightly darker shade of the wall color to create a subtle and sophisticated monochromatic scheme.

24_ Consider alternative trim colors. Instead of the typical arrangement of white trim set against a colored wall, try a dramatic color on your trim.

25_ Look for opportunities to create a contrast between light and dark. A dark wainscot below a bright wall will draw attention to the upper walls, while a bright white wainscot beneath a colored wall will focus the eye on the wainscot.

Paint: Benjamin Moore's Million Dollar Red (above) and Raisin Torte (below)

27

Paint: Valspar's
Jungle Thicket
(woodwork)
and Woodlawn
Misty Morn (walls)

Link spaces with attention-grabbing trim paint. One color for all your woodwork provides a consistent, grounded look, whether in one room or throughout the whole house.

CHAPTER 2

Walls

They are your largest interior canvas—you are literally surrounded by them. And they come in various shapes and sizes. But don't let that overwhelm you. We're here to help. First, we'll explain how to get the perfect paint job—every time. Then the fun really starts. We'll show you how to personalize your walls with everything from stamped and stenciled designs to freehand decorative painting.

Paint: Valspar's Exotic Sea (walls) and
Anthem White (trim)

prep
basics

Prep your walls

→ So you've found the perfect solution for the family room, kitchen, or spare bedroom, and you're ready to pry open that fresh can of paint and get some color on those walls. There's just one thing standing in your way: the room itself. It's not ready yet.

We'll be honest with you: Preparing your surfaces for paint can consume as much as 75 percent of your DIY time. But it's key if you want walls with a flawless finish. Here's how the pros tackle prepping a room for paint.

tools and materials

rosin paper to protect surfaces

drop cloths in canvas and plastic

painter's tape for masking surfaces and taping down paper

screwdriver for removing outlet covers

work lamp to track wall imperfections

1⅝-inch drywall screws for resetting wallboard

drill/driver to drive screws

mini pry bar to remove popped nails

cleaning sponge and **bucket**

degreaser to remove grease, food, grime, and soap residue

putty knife or **painter's 5-in-1 tool**

spackling to fill nail holes and small cracks

joint compound for filling or skimming large areas, either premixed or setting type

pole sander

120-grit and **220-grit silicon-carbide sandpaper**

coarse-grit and **fine-grit sanding sponges**

wet-dry vacuum with broom attachment

caulk gun and **vinyl** or **acrylic adhesive caulk**

2½-inch angled nylon-polyester paintbrush for cutting in along trim

3-inch straight nylon-polyester brush for cutting in where walls meet

9-inch roller frame and **⅜-inch nap roller cover**

all-purpose latex primer-sealer for walls

1 Clear the decks.
Moving everything out might take 15 to 30 minutes more than sliding it to the center of the room, but it makes prep and painting a whole lot easier.

Tip After removing electrical covers, put the screws back on outlets and switches so that they don't get lost.

2 Protect what's left.
Cover floors and fixtures with rosin paper and canvas drop cloths. Plastic ones are fine for covering furniture.

> Remove switch-plate and outlet-receptacle covers and protect switches and outlets with painter's tape.

> As for trim and windowpanes, try to save your tape. Most people overtape, which is time-consuming and can pull off paint if you don't remove it

WARNING:
If your house was built before the 1978 lead-paint ban, have the paint tested before you scrape or sand it. The EPA's website, epa.gov/lead, has guidelines for testing and removal.

before the paint dries. Cutting in with a good brush is easier than you think.

3 Repair any damage.

Shine a work light or bare-bulb lamp across the length of the wall to make any defects jump out. For nail pops, drive a drywall screw into the stud on both sides of the loose fastener, then pry out the nail and patch the hole.

> Fill in dents, small holes, and chipped spots with spackling; it's easy to spread and sand, and the least likely to show under a coat of paint. Because spackling shrinks as it dries, overfill any holes slightly and sand them flush after the filler has hardened.

> Fill deep gouges and large areas of damage with several ¼-inch coats of joint compound or use a setting type that you mix with water; otherwise you'll wind up with a patch that is prone to cracking or that takes forever to dry.

4 Clean all surfaces.

Kitchens and baths require extra attention. Use a degreaser to cut through tough stains from grease, food, and soap. If there's mildew, follow with a 3-to-1 water-to-bleach solution.

5 Sand all surfaces.

Scuff-sand walls with a pole sander armed with 220-grit paper to remove old bumps and to smooth repairs. Wear a dust mask.

> Sand trim with 120-grit sandpaper to level any buildup, feather out the edges of chips, and remove any sheen to provide extra "tooth" for the new coating. A sanding sponge is good for handling the curves on moldings.

6 Beat the dust.

Dust not picked up with a vacuum will find its way back onto the walls. Capture sanding dust with a good shop vacuum. If you can, install a fan in one window to direct free-floating dust outdoors.

> Wipe down ceilings, walls, and trim. Use a damp sponge or lint-free microfiber cloth to pick up sanding dust; rinse and wring them out frequently.

7 Caulk any cracks.

Using a vinyl or acrylic adhesive caulk, run a narrow bead in corner cracks and along every joint where one material meets another.

> For the best control when using caulk, cut a ⅛-inch angled opening in the tube's tip. Break the seal with your caulk gun's puncture tool or use a thin wire so that you don't stretch the nozzle.

> Pull the caulk gun toward you in a smooth motion as you squeeze the trigger, applying only as much as you need.

> Wet your finger and smooth the caulk with even pressure to push it into the crack and leave a smooth edge. Let dry.

8 Prime the walls.

Primers are formulated to remedy surfaces that are too slick, stained, or absorbent for a top coat to stick to or look good. After repairing walls or when making a big color change, prime the entire surface. Use a paintbrush to cut in along trim, corners, and ceiling, then roll the primer on the walls.

> After priming, recheck the walls for any blemishes that need sanding or filling. (Primer can sometimes highlight spots that you overlooked.) Patch as needed and spot-prime once the filler is dry and has been sanded.

49

Wall painting 101

→ The good news: You're in the homestretch. But before you dip that brush or unwrap a new roller, here are some technique and application secrets to ensure your walls and trim get a flawless finish.

Painting walls requires a careful balance between cutting in with a brush—around trim, outlets, inside corners, at the junction of ceiling and wall—and using a roller. It's best to work with a partner, but when painting solo, try to cut in only as much as you can roll while the paint is wet; otherwise you may notice a sheen change in the paint where you switched too late. Be extra vigilant about "hat-banding," a stripe that occurs where the wall meets the ceiling when you don't follow up fast enough with a roller.

tools and materials

2½-inch angled nylon-polyester paintbrush for cutting in along trim and **3-inch straight nylon-polyester brush** for cutting in where walls meet

cut bucket and **liners**

roller frames Both 9-inch and 3-inch frames will be useful.

roller covers Use ⅜-inch nap for smooth walls, ½-inch or longer nap for rougher surfaces.

roller pan and **liners**

extension pole for your roller

step ladder

latex paint See calculator (opposite page) to determine how much you will need.

1 **Cut in around edges.**
Dip a 2½-inch angled brush into a cut bucket, loading it only one-third of the way up the bristles. Use it to cut in a 2- to 3-inch band, against the ceiling and next to molding; switch to a 3-inch brush to cut in where walls meet. Framing in your field this way buffers the roller from adjacent surfaces.

> A loaded brush wants to gush paint, so to start, plant it just back from the edge you're cutting in. Draw the tip up to meet the edge, and drag the brush steadily along it. Reload when the paint starts to fade.

> Before continuing, brush back into the fresh band from the opposite direction to maintain a wet edge and prevent overlap marks. Finish by "tipping off" the area with a light pass in one direction, using only the tip of the almost-dry brush, to minimize brush strokes. Avoid the tendency to keep working the paint back and forth. The object is to apply

Tip Tap off—don't wipe—excess paint on the side of the bucket. This knocks off paint that would cause drips and forces paint into the brush, where it's stored until bristles touch walls or trim.

strokes. Roll up at a slight angle before coming straight down. Steer the roller so that each stroke overlaps half of the previous one. Aim to cover a 3-by-3-foot patch with each rollerful, and finish with a light pass in one direction.

> To prevent paint spray on baseboards when rolling walls, wipe them down with a wet rag so that spatter won't stick. When you've finished rolling, run a damp rag along baseboards to wipe away any drops.

> Continue painting the wall until it's covered. Overlap a bit of the cut-in edges to blend away any visible brush marks. When the roller makes a peeling sound on the wall, it's too dry and needs to be reloaded.

> If you're painting a lot of one color, do as the pros do: Instead of using a pan, fill a 5-gallon bucket with 2 gallons of paint and fit it with a hanging grid. To load your roller, dip it about a quarter of the way into the paint, and roll it against the grid. Repeat until the nap is saturated,

Tip Breathe out while cutting in along trim or where walls meet. It will help you keep a straight line.

it, spread it evenly, smooth it, and move on.

> When cutting in on textured walls, vibrate your hand to get bristle tips into uneven surfaces.

> Consider giving a good brush a lunch break. Latex paint dries very quickly when either the air conditioner or the heater is working. Clean your brush as soon as it starts to feel gummy or heavy—before it starts leaving globs or streaks on your wall.

2 Roll the walls.
Once you've cut in around an entire wall, use a roller to fill in the field. Dampen the roller before using it (use water for latex, paint thinner for oil).

> Dip the roller in a lined tray filled with just enough paint to reach the grate. Roll it back against the grate to distribute the paint and squeeze out the excess. Make sure the roller is covered completely before painting with it.

> To roll the wall, start with a large N or W, then fill in the gaps using short, easy

Tip Before you load a new roller cover, wrap your hand in painter's tape—sticky side out—and pat down the cover to remove any stray fibers.

then press the roller down the grid to spin off excess.

3 And repeat.
Wait an hour after the paint is dry to the touch before applying a second coat.

> When you're done, paint an outlet cover that'll be hidden by furniture and write the name of the color on its back. If you ever have to buy more paint, remove the cover and bring this handy "chip" to the store to get an exact match to the aged version on your walls.

4 Remove tape.
If you've masked off trim with painter's tape, pull it off while the paint is still wet. If you wait, dried paint that bridges the tape and wall may lift off with the tape and damage the finish or surface.

Paint calculator

A gallon of paint covers about 400 square feet. To figure out how much you need, add up the lengths of all your walls, then multiply that sum by the room's height. Subtract 20 square feet for each door and 15 for each window. Divide the result by 400 to get the number of gallons you'll need for one coat. Most walls will need two coats.

$$\left(\substack{\text{LENGTH} \\ \text{OF ALL} \\ \text{WALLS} \\ \text{ADDED} \\ \text{TOGETHER}} \times \substack{\text{HEIGHT} \\ \text{OF} \\ \text{ROOM}} \right) - \substack{20 \\ \text{SQ. FT.} \\ \textit{for each door}} - \substack{15 \\ \text{SQ. FT.} \\ \textit{for each window}} \div 400 = \substack{\text{NUMBER} \\ \text{OF GALLONS} \\ \text{PER COAT}}$$

Multistripe design

→ Broad, even bands of alternating colors deliver a handsome, traditional look. But an accent wall with random-width multicolor stripes? Now that's a paint approach that'll pick up the pace in any room. It'll also provide a host of cheerful shades to echo in your accessories once the paint job is done.

The design shown here might seem as though it doesn't follow a formula, but it's actually a repeating pattern. Five paint colors, and stripes in 1-, 3-, and 5-inch widths, add up to a repeat about 4 feet in length. With a little strategy, though, it can be accomplished with just two rounds of taping and over the course of a couple of days.

Paint: Benjamin Moore's Eccentric Lime, Lucky Charm Green, Splash, Yosemite Blue, and Super White

time Two days
difficulty Moderate to hard. Taping the stripes isn't difficult, but it requires patience and precision.

tools and materials
See what you need to prep your walls, starting on page 48.

tape measure and **color samples** to design the pattern

¼ × 2-inch piece of wood cut to the length of the pattern

4-foot level and **pencil**

1-inch delicate-adhesion painter's tape Double the total number of wall stripes and multiply that number by the height of the wall to determine how much tape you'll need. A roll is about 180 feet long, and you'll need an extra roll or two.

step ladder

plastic putty knife to seal the tape before painting

paint cup and **liners** One per paint color

1-inch and **2½-inch angled nylon-polyester paintbrushes** One per paint color

4-inch mini roller frames and **foam covers** One per paint color

disposable mini roller trays One per paint color

latex paint in five colors for the stripes. Use a premium latex and you may avoid the need for a second coat.

See how to
prep the wall
for paint,
page 48.

1

Design the
repeating pattern

> Create a pattern of stripe widths and colors to repeat across the wall (the pattern here is about 4 feet wide). This brings visual order to the sequence of stripes and makes the project manageable.

> To design the pattern, cut samples of each paint color into strips equal to the desired width of the stripes, such as 1, 3, and 5 inches, as shown. Your pattern can have any number of colors, but they should complement one another when viewed as a whole. We chose five colors.

Tip Including white in the stripe pattern is a good way to break up the color sequence and give the eye a rest.

online helper
Download a template for this design at
thisoldhouse.com/books

2

Create a story stick

> Rather than fumbling with a measuring tape, cut a thin strip of lumber the length of one full stripe sequence and measure off and mark the stripes' boundaries.

> Use 1-inch painter's tape to extend each line evenly around the stick—this will make it easier to transfer your markings. The width of the tape itself will mark the 1-inch stripe. Be sure to keep the tape to the same sides of the lines, and, for good measure, draw an arrow indicating which edge of each tape wrap serves as the line.

> Label the left and right ends of the stick, as well as the color for each stripe, to remind you how to orient it each time you pick it back up.

3

Mark the wall and transfer the lines

> Hold the story stick against the project wall with the left end abutting the adjacent wall. Align it with a level, then transfer the pattern lines onto the wall with light tick marks (A). When you reach the end of the stick, circle the last tick mark so that you know where to start the stick on the next sequence.

> Using a 4-foot level, draw the stripes' boundaries with light pencil marks at the top, middle, and bottom of the wall (B). Be mindful that pencil can peek through even dark paint.

A **B**

4

Tape off the stripes

> On the first round, you'll tape off and paint every other stripe and let them dry. For Round 2, you'll mask along the edges of the painted stripes to bracket off the unpainted ones.

> Before you start, put X's of painter's tape over the stripes you want to skip. Then, from a step ladder, start at the top of each stripe and work your way down, taping off along both borders of the stripes to be painted. Let the tape extend at the floor and ceiling for easy removal.

> Draw arrows on the tape pointing toward the area to be painted.

> Run a plastic putty knife down each strip of tape as you work to ensure that the tape edges fully adhere to the wall (a metal blade could mar the wall). This will keep the paint from bleeding underneath.

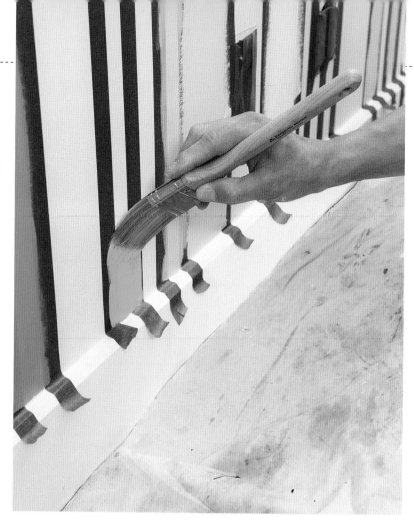

5

Paint the first set of stripes

> On the first round, you'll paint the stripes between the arrows.

> Using a paintbrush, cut in along the ceiling and baseboard, and along the wall adjacent to the first stripe.

> For skinny stripes, stick with the paintbrush for the entire length. When painting with the brush, keep your strokes vertical and pull away from the tape to avoid pushing paint beneath it.

> For large stripes, use a small roller to coat the open area between the tape. Again, use vertical strokes to prevent paint bleed.

A

B

6

Switch the tape

> Remove the tape before the paint dries. Otherwise, removing the tape may remove paint, too. Start at the ceiling and pull downward at an angle (A).

> After the paint on the first set of stripes has dried for at least 24 hours, tape off the second set of stripes by aligning tape on the edges of each painted stripe (B). Seal the tape with a plastic putty knife.

7

Paint the second set of stripes

> Cut in and paint the remaining stripes with a brush or roller, removing the tape while the paint is still wet.

Tip Hold the story stick up to the wall as a reference before you paint each stripe to ensure you're using the right color.

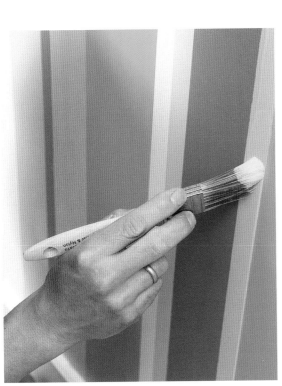

8

Touch up the stripes

> Once the paint is dry, carefully touch up any gaps or overlaps with a brush. Create a clean line by holding the brush at a 45-degree angle away from the wall, as shown, then press the tip of the brush to the wall and steadily guide it toward the line. Run the paintbrush along the line until the gap is coated.

IDEA FILE

There are dozens of ways to reinterpret this multistripe design. Here are a few that we love

Young and hip
All-white decor turns a striped accent wall into a room-size work of art. Bands of strong color in a handful of sizes is a design that works well in a kid's room or a modern living space. Paint: Sherwin-Williams' Black Bean, Dynamic Blue, Gypsy Red, Eastlake Gold, and Eros

Subdued sophistication
A fireplace bumpout is a natural for an accent wall of horizontal stripes. To keep the design subtle, choose muted, closely related colors and incorporate large bands of the base color. Paint: Glidden's Silver Night (base coat), Coastal Blue, Innocence, Obsidian Glass, and Cozy Light

Bright border
A riot of lively stripes in a repeating pattern rings tall wainscot in this black-and-white bath. The color scheme is reinforced, but not overwhelmed, by painting the interior of the storage cubbies in the same six shades.
Paint: Behr's Ultra Pure White, Flame Yellow, Red Tomato, Ocean Cruise, Lightweight Beige, and Crisp Apple

ALTERNATE TECHNIQUE: ROLLER STRIPES

Grab a mini roller and a paint tray to make easy, informal stripes with a freehand-painted look. Here's how:

> Paint the base color; let dry.

> Wrap a thick rubber band around the center of a 5-inch foam roller cover. Wrap it tightly so that the center of the cover doesn't touch the wall while you're rolling.

> Dip the roller in the paint tray and practice your roller stripes on paper first. You can add another rubber band to make the stripes thinner, if you like.

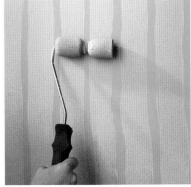

> On the wall, roll the stripes in one pass from top to bottom in order to keep them smooth and continuous.

Paint: Glidden's Malabar (base coat) and Lavender Twilight (stripes)

Showpiece
Wide stripes are a great way to frame a favorite piece of furniture, creating a mini accent wall. The gray and pink bands here nicely play off the louvered look of the front of this credenza. Paint: Ralph Lauren Paint's Avalanche (base coat), Sweatshirt Grey, and Temptation

Playfully skinny
No repeat here. Vertical stripes painted in a variety of sizes and colors inject a fun feel into this family room. Paint: Valspar's Sapphire 5, Lemon Twist, Autumn Blaze, Afternoon Delight, Clean White, Berry Blush, Pink Plunge, Gleeful, Fairmont Penthouse Garnet, and Homecoming Blue

Added drama
Thick horizontal stripes exaggerate the curves of this stairwell. Bright-colored outlines on the muted lavender, cream, and tan bands increase the sense of movement even more. Paint: Behr's Lilac Bisque, China Cup, Quiet Refuge, Country Breeze, Whimsical White, Poinsettia, Tropical Splash, Finesse, and Twenty Carat

High and wide
Yellow and white bands of equal width climbing up the walls and onto the ceiling create a tentlike effect that's comfortably cozy in a bedroom. Paint: Valspar's Soft Duckling and Clean White

Vintage pinstripe
Thin apple-green horizontal stripes give white bedroom walls a paneled look. The bottom band of vertical stripes even creates a subtle wainscot. Paint: Sherwin-Williams' Pure White and Baize Gecko

Linen and denim effects

 Dragging, or strié, is a way to add a veneer of texture to smooth surfaces by pulling a dry brush through a wet layer of tinted glaze. It's as versatile as you are patient and creative, producing looks from subtle to striking. Contrast between the base coat and glaze color pronounces the effect, while layered tones of similar intensity provide a rich luster.

A crisscross pattern like the one on the wainscot here takes on the look of fabric, though the choice and combination of colors dresses down what might otherwise be a formal treatment. In fact, layering three shades of blue gives the wall a depth of character not unlike your favorite jeans. The brown and white hues of the upper wall could pass for linen, with the chair rail tying everything together like a crisp white belt.

[ESSENTIAL TOOL]
DRAGGING BRUSH
No need to spring for a pricey pro brush with fine bristles that might mush the glaze. Look for something stiff and coarse, like a whisk broom, scrub brush, or this wallpaper paste brush with the soft tips lopped off.

time Two days, counting drying time between glaze coats

difficulty Moderate to hard. Striating the glaze is easy enough, but you must work quickly and move smoothly and steadily to produce an even pattern. Practice—or a partner—helps.

tools and materials
See what you need to prep your walls and paint the base coats, starting on page 48.

2½-inch angled nylon-polyester paintbrush to cut in along trim

9-inch roller frame

⅜-inch nap roller cover Get one for each layer of glaze.

paint tray and **liners**

dragging brush or **any stiff-bristle brush** at least 4 inches wide to create striations in the glaze

clean rags or **paper towel**

two disposable cups and **wide-mouth container** for mixing the glaze and paint

clear acrylic latex glaze to create semitranslucent, luminous top coats with extended working time

latex paint in five colors: two for the upper walls, three for the wainscot. Using a satin, or glossier, paint for the base coat makes it easier to redo any mistakes with the glaze.

Paint: Behr's Ashwood (base coat) and Ultra Pure White (glaze coat) on upper wall; Cornflower Blue (base coat), Starless Night (vertical glaze coat), and Mesmerize (horizontal glaze coat) below

See how to prep for and paint the **perfect base coat,** page 48.

1

Mix the glaze

> Once the base coat on the upper walls is dry, use disposable cups to mix equal parts glaze and the first top-coat color. Stir. Pour into a paint tray.

2

Roll glaze on the upper walls

> Beginning at the top corner of one wall, cut in and roll the glaze in a strip from ceiling to chair rail. Don't make it wider than 3 feet, to ensure that the glaze won't dry before you drag it. For large walls, you may need to enlist a partner so that one person can roll on the glaze while the other follows behind with the dragging brush.

3

Drag the glaze vertically

> Press your dragging brush into the glaze at the top corner of the wall and pull down. The bristles will cut grooves through the glaze to expose the base color. Continue in one uninterrupted stroke to the chair rail. On the next round, overlap the first dragged area slightly to avoid a visible seam (A).

> Use a clean rag or paper towel to wipe excess glaze off the brush regularly (B).

TIP Hang plumb bobs—you can make your own by tying washers to household twine—just off the wall for a visual guide as you apply the vertical strokes.

4

Roll and drag the wainscot vertically

> When the wainscot base color is dry, mix glaze with the first top-coat color, as in Step 1.

> Starting at the top of one corner, cut in and then roll on a band of glaze between the chair rail and baseboard.

> Drag your dry brush through the wet glaze, pulling steadily from top to bottom without stopping. (This smaller expanse makes it a good project for beginners.)

> Roll the next patch, overlapping the dragged area by several inches. Repeat.

5

Then roll and drag it horizontally

> After letting the first dragged layer dry completely—a day should do it—mix glaze with the second top-coat color, as in Step 1.

> Apply the glaze in a manageable strip running the full length of the wall beneath the chair rail, side to side. You may need to roll on the glaze vertically and horizontally to penetrate the grooves of your first layer.

> Starting at one corner, drag the glaze across the wainscot, again taking care not to stop until you get to the far wall.

> Roll the next strip, overlapping the first slightly, and repeat till the wainscot is complete.

Tip If you don't like the results of a particular pass, don't fret—simply reroll the area and begin again. This is the beauty of using glaze, which extends the drying time of your paint.

Stamped geometrics

→ Remember those potato stamps you made in grade school? Now imagine a less starchy—but no less fun—medium made with a sheet of flexible craft foam and squares of scrap wood. Two homemade stamps and semi-gloss paint made the pattern shown here—a great way to add energy to a small area. The end result is a look that's akin to handmade wallpaper.

The pattern here is kept loose by moving the diamond-within-a-square stamp across the wall in freehand fashion, with smaller circles in between. Try out your stamps on a piece of colored paper first. Experiment by varying the amount of paint you load on them till you get a look you like.

time Two days
difficulty Easy. Just be sure to practice on paper first.

tools and materials
See what you need to prep your walls and paint the base coat, starting on page 48.

pencil and **scrap paper** for figuring out your shapes

craft foam in sheets or precut shapes (available at craft stores)

utility knife if you're cutting out shapes

wood glue

scrap wood blocks to make your stamps. A block less than 5 inches square and about 1 inch thick fits comfortably in an adult hand. Sand the edges.

disposable plastic plates to hold the paint. You want to use it up in small amounts before it dries out.

small artist's brush

damp sponge to clean up any mistakes

latex paint in two colors. Choose a semigloss for the stamping, which will contrast best over a flat base coat.

Paint: Benjamin Moore's Hawthorne Yellow (base coat) and White Dove (stamp)

1

Create the stamps

> Figure out shapes by drawing a pattern on paper. Here, a 1-inch circle and 4-inch square were cut out of craft foam, then glued to wood blocks. A diamond with four equal sides was drawn on the square and cut out with a utility knife.

See how to prep for and paint the **perfect base coat,** page 48.

2

Apply the paint

> Once the base coat is dry, pour stamping paint onto a disposable plastic plate. Dip the stamp into the paint to load it, or use a small artist's brush to cover the foam's surface (A).

> Practice stamping on paper. As you get a feel for it, adjust the amount of paint on the stamp and the pressure you're using. Don't press so hard that you extract every bit of paint—you want it somewhat uneven (B).

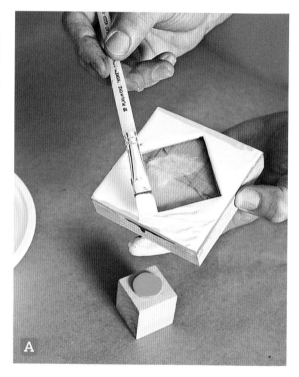

A

B

How to find a pattern

So you've found the perfect wall for stamping but are unsure about what to stamp? Here are some places to look for inspiration to create just the right stamped design.

> **Go to the bookstore or your local library.** There are plenty of books solely dedicated to patterns. You can find source books on Japanese, Scandinavian, and Early American patterns, as well as nature-based and geometric designs.

> **Look online.** Search clip-art sites for a treasure trove of interesting patterns and shapes. Many of the illustrations are black and white, so they can easily be converted to a pattern that's simple to stamp.

> **Simplify a complicated design.** Look within an intricate pattern for shapes that you like, such as a single flower within a damask pattern. These will translate more easily to a stamp design.

3

Press the stamp flat to the wall

> Move across the wall in horizontal rows. Here, every other 4-inch square was stamped. If you're worried about wavy lines, let a chalk line be your guide. Adjust spacing when you near the end of a row so that you finish with a full square. Keep a damp sponge handy to clean up any mistakes.

4

Center circles in blank squares

> Gently press with the dot stamp to avoid thick, solid dots—you want a bit of the base coat to show through. Don't worry too much about placement. It's a small stamp, so if it's off a little bit it'll still look fine.

pro advice

BRIAN CARTER,
DECORATIVE PAINTER

"For a softer look, lower the contrast of the colors and finishes. If you want more energy, crank up the contrast—semigloss yellow on flat navy, for example."

5

Touch up thin spots

> Use a small artist's brush to add a little more paint where the coverage seems too meager or a lot of the outline of the pattern is missing.

○ IDEA FILE

Stamping is a great way to give a
sophisticated wallpaper feel to a room
without the mess of paper and paste

Subtle shimmer
A field of lilac takes on the appearance of a high-end
wall covering with an off-the-shelf medallion stamp
and silver paint. Paint: Sherwin-Williams' Breathtaking
(base coat) and FolkArt's Metallic Silver (stamp)

Block-print look
Deep red paisleys repeated
across a sage green wall
get a lot of variation from a
single ready-made stamp.
Paint: C2 Paint's Saguaro
(base coat) and FolkArt's
Terracotta (stamp)

Tip To avoid rigid rows
while creating an evenly
spaced pattern on the wall,
tie a pencil to a string and
knot the end. Place the
knot at the center of your
first medallion and mark
the center of the next one
with the pencil—and so on.

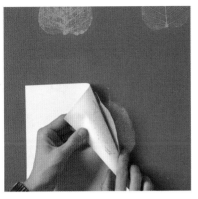

ALTERNATE TECHNIQUE: LEAF STAMPING

Step outside to gather supplies for this one-of-a-kind design.

> Paint your wall with a base coat of your choice. Let dry. Collect a handful of leaves; the ones used here have the same basic size and shape. They should be pliable, not brittle.

> Run craft glue (or double-stick tape) down the center of each leaf. Affix it to a sheet of white paper and let dry. Tuck paper towel under the leaf's edges, then use a small foam brush to thinly coat the leaf with acrylic craft paint in a color that offers some contrast to the base.

> Remove the paper towel, and press the paper-backed leaf to the wall. Don't move or twist the leaf—the design will smear. Continue the process, following a pattern or randomly scattering leaves across your wall.

Paint: Valspar's Wishing Well (base coat) and Lumiere's Metallic Sunset Gold (stamp)

Two-tone color wash

→ You could spend days with a float and a trowel trying to make your marred plaster walls look perfect. But where's the fun in that? You'd be much better off just embracing the old plaster's rough surface and faded color. Or maybe you live in a new house and would love to infuse your too-pristine drywall with a little old-world character. In either case, painting on a two-tone color wash can warm up your walls with an aged look.

With a few brushes and a pair of complementary hues thinned with glaze, you can mimic wall color created long before the paint roller came along. This technique will hide surface imperfections—or create them intentionally where walls are too smooth. What you'll end up with when you're done is a look so delightfully imperfect, it's perfect.

Paint: Ralph Lauren Paint's Chesapeake Sunset (base coat), Hunter Orange (first glaze coat), and Yellowhammer (second glaze coat)

→

time 10 hours over two days

difficulty Easy. But it does require a resilient arm to apply several coats of paint.

tools and materials
See what you need to prep your walls and paint the base coat, starting on page 48.

cut bucket and **liners**

two 2½-inch nylon-polyester paintbrushes

4-inch polyester paintbrush to dry-brush the finish

paper towels to dry off brush bristles

clear acrylic latex glaze to create semitranslucent, luminous top coats with extended working time

latex paint in three colors: a semigloss base coat and two colors in eggshell or matte to layer on top. Since the top coats get mixed with glaze, get about half as much of these colors as you would need to paint the whole room.

See how to prep for and paint the **perfect base coat,** page 48.

1

Brush on the first color

> Once the base coat is dry, take a lined cut bucket and mix the darker of the two top-coat paint colors with the glaze, 2 parts paint to 1 part glaze. Stir thoroughly.

> Using a 2½-inch nylon-polyester paintbrush, brush the color onto the wall. Begin by marking a large X in the middle of the wall (A). Without refilling your brush, sweep smaller, random marks across and over the X to drag and spread the glaze (B). Dip the brush in the glaze again as it begins to dry, and continue the choppy, random brush strokes until you've covered the wall in a pattern of haphazard marks. Be sure to leave a lot of the base color showing through.

A   B

2

Cut in along the edges

> Wherever the walls meet the trim or the ceiling, use the brush to create a clean edge line. Position the bristle tips a fraction of an inch from the molding or ceiling color, then gently flick the brush toward the center of the wall you're working on, using short strokes.

> Continue along the edge, staggering the angles and length of your strokes as you go until the perimeter is filled in. Once the walls are complete, allow the first-layer color to dry.

3

Brush on the second color

> Fit the cut bucket with a fresh liner and mix the second top-coat color with glaze in the same 2-to-1 proportions you used for the first top-coat color.

> Using a fresh 2½-inch paintbrush, brush the glaze onto the wall, working in a small area. Apply it with the same choppy, random strokes and cutting-in technique you used with the first glaze coat.

TIP Step back from the wall frequently to check that you're covering the space evenly. Go back and fix bare spots as needed.

4

Dry-brush the finish

> As you apply the second top coat, stop every 3 feet or so and, using a dry 4-inch polyester brush, sweep the wet glaze with the tips of the bristles to blend and soften the effect. Work in long, broad strokes; the more you dry-brush, the more the brush marks will fade. Be careful not to brush the effect away completely.

> Stop occasionally to wash excess glaze off the brush. Dry it off by brushing it over several paper towels.

○ ALTERNATE TECHNIQUES

Different color-wash effects can be accomplished with a variety of simple, inexpensive "tools," including sponges, rags, and even plastic sacks. By either applying or removing top layers of paint, they allow you to play with light and depth to great effect. Note: For all these hands-on methods, you'll want the protection of a pair of disposable gloves

Sponging on
DRAMATIC TEXTURE

> Once the base coat is dry, mix equal parts glaze and a top-coat color. Mask off any areas you don't want to sponge. Wet a large sea sponge, wring it out, and dip it in the glaze. Squeeze out any excess and use the loaded sponge to cut in at the top left corner of the wall. Continue, patting it against the wall in a random pattern, working out from the corner, top to bottom. The glaze should go on thick and textured but shouldn't drip. The base coat color should still come through.

Paint: Behr's Dark Storm Cloud (base coat) and Wine Barrel (glaze coat)

Tip For a more faceted treatment, like the rusted-steel look shown at right, sponge on a third color after the second dries.

Paint: Behr's Cracked Pepper (second glaze coat)

[ESSENTIAL TOOL]
SEA SPONGE
A large natural sea sponge with a good scattering of holes in different sizes allows you to vary the pattern simply by turning it.

Rag rolling off
A WARM, MOTTLED LOOK

> Once the base coat is dry, mix equal parts glaze with a color at least two shades lighter (or darker) than the wall color. Cut in with a brush at the top left corner, then roll on a generous coat of the glaze in an area only about 4 by 4 feet so that you can texture it before it dries. This is easier with two people: one to roll on the color, one to rag-roll it off.

> Press a crumpled plastic grocery sack into the wet glaze and tumble it back and forth along overlapping angles. The wrinkles will pull away the glaze in a scattered impression of swirls, exposing the lighter base coat beneath. Work the same area until you achieve the desired effect. Then glaze an adjacent area, overlapping the edge of the first, and repeat.

Paint: Sherwin-Williams' Lounge Green (base coat) and Benjamin Moore's Nile Green (glaze coat)

Tip Before working directly on your walls, first try out your technique on cardboard coated with your base color.

Ragging on

A SOFT,
DAPPLED EFFECT

> Once the base coat is dry, mix equal parts glaze and your top-coat color. Mask off any areas you don't want to rag, but there's no need to cut in.

> Take a clean cotton rag, saturate it with the glaze, and wring it out. Pile it into one hand, making sure to tuck in any loose ends. Holding the wadded-up bundle lightly, dab at the wall to apply glaze directly to the base coat. Don't press it into the wall. You want an even, dappled look. Re-crumple the rag every so often or whenever you notice an identical pattern showing up.

Paint: Glidden's Deepest Aqua (base coat) and European White (glaze coat)

Tip For a slightly more diffuse texture, you can use dye-free paper towels instead of a cloth rag.

Stenciled accent border

→ In colonial times, allover stenciled patterns of flowers or fruit were a frugal way to approximate pricey hand-printed wallpaper. Today, stenciling is still an inexpensive way to add charm to a room. Even if you've never worked with stencils, painting an accent border around a doorway is a project any novice can tackle.

The toughest part of this project might just be deciding on a design. Do you want a border that's architectural and geometric, or a naturalistic pattern like leaves and vines? Let the room's style be your guide. There are plenty of precut stencils you can work with, but to create a custom look—and fit—for your space, consider designing and making your own, as we did here. Dab on paint very lightly, so that the base coat shows through, for a look that's both old-world and up-to-date.

[ESSENTIAL TOOL]
STENCIL BRUSH
The flat tip helps you apply the paint with a dabbing motion so that it doesn't get underneath the stencil. Brushes come in many sizes; choose one that suits your stencil's scale and shape.

Paint: Benjamin Moore's Chameleon (base coat) and Oatmeal (stencil)

time 6 hours
difficulty Easy to moderate. Designing the pattern and cutting out the stencils takes patience and precision, but the painting is a cinch.

tools and materials
See what you need to prep your walls and paint the base coat, starting on page 48.

measuring tape

yardstick or **ruler** and **pencil**

delicate-adhesion painter's tape

stencil film This is also called template plastic or acetate.

self-healing cutting mat

fine-tip permanent marker

X-Acto knife

electric stencil-cutting pen (available at craft stores) for cutting curved lines into the stencil, and **a pane of glass**

repositionable mounting spray

plastic putty knife to smooth the stencil in place

old newspapers

paper plate or **mini roller tray** for holding the paint

flat-tip stencil brush We used one with a ⅝-inch diameter.

lint-free cloths or **sturdy paper towels** for cleaning stencils and prepping the stencil brush

latex paint in two colors Choose a flat or satin finish for both the base coat and the stencil to achieve a timeworn look.

See how to prep for and paint the **perfect base coat,** page 48.

1

Lay out the border

> When the base coat is dry, measure the length of the casing above the doorway. Mark a centerline on the casing (A). You'll use this mark later to help position the top stencil.

> Sketch a pattern freehand or print one using a computer. Affix your pattern to the wall with painter's tape, leaving a consistent space between the edge of the casing and your stencil design (B). Lightly mark each end of the border on the wall with a pencil.

online helper
Download a template for this design at **thisoldhouse.com/books**

2

Trace the pattern onto stencil film

> This border required four stencils: a top detail, a corner detail, a tail detail, and a linear pattern to connect them. On a work surface, lay a piece of stencil film over the top detail, aligning it with the edge of the pattern that's closest to the door casing. Cut the film to size, leaving a space of at least 1 inch all the way around the pattern to keep the stencil intact.

> Tape the film to your sketch to prevent shifting, and trace the pattern onto the film with a fine-tip permanent marker using a ruler or yardstick as needed. Trace remaining stencils in the same manner. Measure and mark a centerline on the bottom edge of the top stencil.

3

Cut the stencils

> To cut straight lines, place the film and pattern on top of a self-healing cutting mat. Using an X-Acto knife guided by a ruler or yardstick, cut carefully along the lines (A).

> To cut curved lines, place the film and pattern on top of a pane of glass to protect your work surface from the electric stencil-cutting pen. Carefully trace the cut lines with the tip of the pen, working in small sections and lifting the pen from the film as needed to keep the cuts crisp (B).

Tip When cutting out stencils, pull the X-Acto knife or cutting pen toward you as you work, for a clean cut.

4

Position the top stencil

> Lay the top stencil facedown on several sheets of newspaper. Apply a light coating of repositionable mounting spray on the back of the stencil. Allow it to dry for several minutes or until the adhesive feels tacky.

> Holding the stencil away from the wall, align its centerline with the one you marked on the door casing in Step 1. Working from the center outward, press the stencil into place. Use a plastic putty knife to smooth it out; this will remove air bubbles and prevent paint from bleeding underneath.

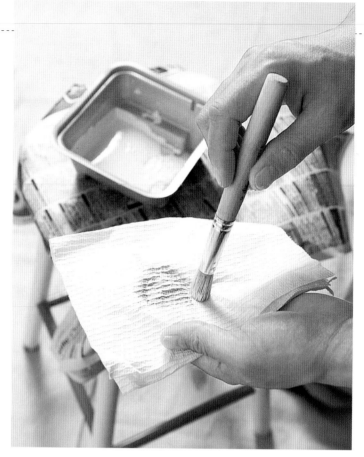

5

Prep your brush

> Pour paint into a small container. Dip the end of a flat-tip stencil brush in the paint, then lightly dab the ends of the bristles on a lint-free cloth or paper towel, leaving the brush nearly dry.

6

Paint the top detail

> Using a dabbing motion, pounce the paint in the open areas of the stencil (A). Use a very light touch near the ends of the stencil where the pattern will continue, to prevent any visible, overpainted seams. Continue until the pattern is filled in but the wall color underneath still shows through.

> When you're finished, carefully pull up one corner of the stencil, then peel it away from the wall at a sharp angle (B).

Tip Avoid bending the stencil brush's bristles with a sweeping motion. This can leave brush marks and cause paint to bleed beneath the stencil.

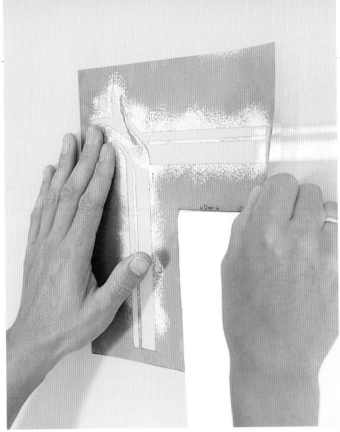

7

Continue the pattern

> Repeat Steps 4, 5, and 6, working your way outward from the top stencil. Overlap each stencil with the previous pattern, but avoid overpainting those seams. And let the paint dry before mounting the next stencil.

> Between uses, rinse stencils in hot water and dry with a lint-free cloth or paper towel. Flip over the corner stencil to paint the symmetrical pattern at the doorway's opposite corner.

8

Complete the border

> Mount the tail stencil on one side of the doorway as described in Step 4. Paint the pattern as described in Steps 5 and 6. Rinse and dry the stencil, then flip it over and repeat on the opposite side.

○IDEA FILE

Take stenciled details to a whole new level with graphic designs that unfurl across the wall. Play with repeating patterns or opt for a single accent piece to instantly personalize your space

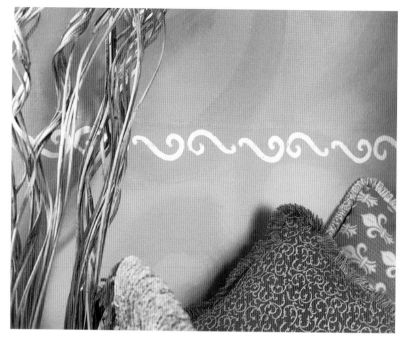

Sunny swirls
Snaking across the center of a wall in a naturally imperfect line, lemon-hued curlicues offer the same visual impact as a chair rail—and help break up an expanse of bright orange.
Paint: Pratt & Lambert's Burnished Gold (base coat) and Dutch Gold (stencil)

Blooming branches
A spray of cherry blossoms brings a hint of spring indoors and enlivens neutral walls. Even the room's bed becomes part of the motif, with fabric paint used to extend the design onto the upholstered headboard. Paint: Sherwin-Williams' Fiery Brown (branches), and Mauve Finery and Cheery (flowers)

Panel effect
Turn a garden-variety wall recess into the center of attention by painting it with a vibrant block of color, then layering it with a bold stenciled floral pattern in a pale shade. Paint: Glidden's Summer Picnic (base coat), Quiet Knoll (panel), and Pure White (stencil)

One feathery flourish
Writ large, a single wispy peacock plume has a dramatic impact. To achieve a similar ombré effect, start painting the top of the stencil pale blue, then work your way down, using gradually deeper shades until the stem is an inky indigo. Paint: Olympic's Violet Shadow (base coat), and Crashing Waves, Fresh Water, Stormy Ridge, and Dark As Night (stencil)

A faded field
Painted the same creamy white as
the furniture, a sprightly row of
cloudlike blossoms draws the eye
upward and unifies the room. Paint:
Glidden's Blue Collar (base coat)
and White High-Hiding (stencil)

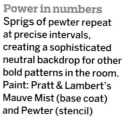

Power in numbers
Sprigs of pewter repeat
at precise intervals,
creating a sophisticated
neutral backdrop for other
bold patterns in the room.
Paint: Pratt & Lambert's
Mauve Mist (base coat)
and Pewter (stencil)

Showered with petals
Who needs a bed of roses when you can sleep
beneath a canopy of flowering branches? Here, the
stencils are arrayed to frame the headboard's exotic
shape while echoing its neutral hue. Paint: Pratt &
Lambert's Samovar (base coat) and Pro White (stencils)

Understated elegance
With their delicate lines
and subtle color play, these
flower stencils make a
clever, and inexpensive,
stand-in for luxe wallpaper.
Paint: Behr's Sandstone
Cove (base coat), and
Maiden Voyage (stencils)

Distinguished panels
Forget large works of framed art: Create your own with stenciled wall panels. In this room, three crisp blocks of deep-green highlight the homeowner's collection of all-white accessories—and also provide the backdrop for a pair of intricate garden motifs. Paint: Valspar's Clean White (base coat, stencil) and French Olive (panels)

Stippled stripes

→ Stippling offers a delicate way to soften the impact of a large expanse of color. The micro-suedelike texture is created by pouncing a flat, square brush against a freshly glazed surface. The bristles lift away the colored glaze to expose the base color, but the freckles are so tiny that from a distance your eye blends them into one shade. You could say that the technique adds a lovely haziness to the color.

Precisely because the effect is subtle, you may want to put it to work in a striped pattern to play it up a bit. Here, we used 2-inch painter's tape over the base coat to create our 2-inch-thick white stripes and simply stippled between them. Suddenly a formerly white wall gets a sophisticated cottage look.

[ESSENTIAL TOOL]
STIPPLING BRUSH
Stippling really is easier with a dedicated, densely bristled brush. You can spend $300 on one, but a $30 version will do fine. Save even more by making your own from a bunch of chip brushes (see page 20).

Paint: Benjamin Moore's Super White (base coat) and Behr's Silver Tinsel (glaze coat)

time 6 hours
difficulty Easy. Measuring and taping the pattern takes time, but the stippling itself goes fast once you get into a rhythm.

tools and materials
See what you need to prep your walls and paint the base coat, starting on page 48.

2-inch delicate-adhesion painter's tape to lay out the stripes

4-foot level and **pencil** to create guides for the stripes

plastic putty knife to seal the tape before painting

2½-inch nylon-polyester paintbrush

stippling brush to create the finish

clean, dry rag to wipe glaze off the stippling brush

two disposable cups for measuring paint and glaze

cut bucket and **liner**

latex paint in two colors, one for the base coat, one for the glaze coat

clear acrylic latex glaze to create a semitranslucent, luminous top coat with an extended working time

See how to prep for and paint the **perfect base coat,** page 48.

1

Lay out the stripes, brush on the glaze

> Run 2-inch painter's tape along the top of the wall, sealing the edges with a plastic putty knife; this will be the narrow, base-coat-color stripe. Measure and mark a spot 4 inches below the bottom of the tape; extend a line from this point with tick marks across the wall using a level. This will be the wide, stippled stripe. Line up the tape with the tick marks to create the next narrow stripe. And so on, to finish the pattern.

> Using two disposable cups, mix equal parts of the top-coat color and glaze in a lined cut bucket. Starting at the left side of the top stripe, brush on a section of glaze about 4 feet wide.

pro advice
MARK POWERS,
TOH SENIOR TECHNICAL EDITOR

MEASURING OPTION
"To get the pattern to finish evenly, angle a tape measure from ceiling to baseboard until it lands on a number divisible by one pairing of stripes—here, it's 6 inches. Now simply mark along the tape at 6, 12, 18 inches and so on, to get an even spacing of tick marks to guide your taping."

2

Stipple the glaze

> Working quickly so that the glaze doesn't set up, pounce the stippling brush evenly across the wet surface. You should see the base coat begin to peek through where the bristles lift the glaze—it's a subtle effect but clearly visible up close.

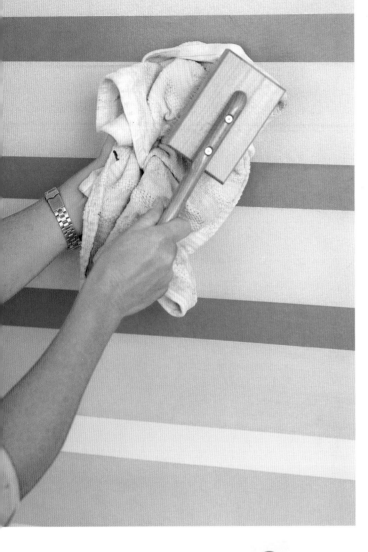

3

Finish the remaining stripes

> Before moving on, use a clean, dry rag to wipe glaze off your brush. Repeat this step as necessary throughout the process; if the brush is overloaded, you'll be splashing, not stippling.

> Apply glaze to the next section of stripe, slightly overlapping the already textured part, and stipple it in the same way. Work left to right, top to bottom.

> When you're finished, remove the tape while the glaze is still tacky to prevent the top coat from being pulled off.

Tip When choosing a color to mix with the glaze, keep in mind how much it will lighten or darken your base coat.

Moroccan star design

→ Looking for an out-of-the-ordinary paint pattern for your walls? Try borrowing from a ceramic tile design. That was the inspiration for the curvy Moroccan stars that cover this bedroom accent wall. Simplifying and blowing up the pattern keeps it from being fussy. Interrupting it along the ceiling and at the corners keeps it from appearing too rigid.

The secret to hand-painting what looks like a complicated pattern is using two templates. Think paper snowflake: Fold a couple of squares of posterboard into quarters, sketch along the unfolded edges, then cut along the outlines. Unfold, and you should have two symmetrical shapes. Place one template at a time on the wall and outline it in chalk until your pattern is complete. Then put the templates away and paint freehand right over the chalk lines.

Paint: Benjamin Moore's Palladian Blue (base coat) and Standish White (design), and FolkArt's Metallic Solid Bronze (dots)

→

time Two days
difficulty Moderate, once you master painting the curves. To get comfortable loading the brush and painting freehand, practice on posterboard first.

tools and materials
See what you need to prep your walls and paint the base coat, starting on page 48.

chalk line, yardstick and **pencil** to create a grid on the wall

scrap paper to draft a design

posterboard and **scissors** to create the templates

white blackboard chalk

½-inch round artist's brush

latex paint in two colors. We used an eggshell finish for the base coat and semigloss for the pattern.

acrylic craft paint for the dots

damp sponge to erase chalk lines

1

Mark a diagonal grid on the wall in chalk

> Once the base coat is dry, measure the wall side to side and snap a chalk line down its center from ceiling to baseboard. Snap more lines to the left and right of this centerline at 18-inch intervals until you hit the corners. About 3 inches from the ceiling, mark the bottom of the top row of interrupted stars, using chalk. From there, move down the chalk lines, marking dots at 18-inch intervals.

> Use a yardstick to connect the dots diagonally and create a grid of 18-by-18-inch diamonds.

See how to prep for and paint the **perfect base coat,** page 48.

2

Make the large star template

> Practice sketching the large star pattern on scrap paper until you have a version you like. Cut out a piece of posterboard 18 inches square. Fold into quarters to form a triangle.

> With a pencil, copy one-quarter of the star outline along the unfolded edge (A). Cut along the outline with scissors (B). Unfold; you should have a large equal-sided template (C).

A

B

C

→ **online helper**
Download templates for this design at **thisoldhouse.com/books**

3

Outline the large stars with chalk

> Placing the big template under one of the topmost dots, use chalk to outline a column of whole stars. Continue, working down in vertical columns along the chalk lines.

> Outline the interrupted stars at the wall's top, bottom, and corners, bending the template as needed to make outlining easier.

4

Make the small star template

> Cut out a piece of posterboard 6 inches square. Fold it in quarters to form a triangle.

> Draw one-quarter of the small star along the unfolded edge. Cut along the outline with scissors (A). Unfold; you should have a small equal-sided template (B).

Tip Find inspiration for a custom pattern by looking in one of the many books devoted to ceramic tile design.

5

Trace the inner pattern

> Center the smaller template within one of the topmost full-size stars and outline it with chalk. Continue, working down in vertical columns. Notice that the spaces between your large stars create a separate set of stars that don't get small stars. You should end up with a pattern that has an equal number of two-template and one-template stars.

A

B

Tip Avoid choosing very-high-contrast colors for the base coat and star pattern. That way, small imperfections won't show.

6

Paint the design

> Using a ½-inch round artist's brush, paint the large stars right over the chalk outlines in a color that provides a soft contrast with the wall (A). Make sure the stars touch at all four points. Let dry.

> Now paint the small stars over their chalk outlines (B). Let dry.

7

Add the accent dots

> Using the same brush and an accent color, such as this bronze, paint dots at the intersections of all the large stars. (We used an acrylic latex craft paint that comes in a convenient small size.) Let dry; add a second coat if needed.

8

Wipe away the chalk

> Once the dots are fully dry, use a damp sponge to erase the chalk grid and any visible chalk marks.

Freehand twig pattern

→ Wall-frame molding can help make a large room feel more intimate, but those rectangles can be a challenge to work with. You need just-the-right-size artwork to hang within the rigid structure. So why not make your own art? Try this project of delicately painted tree branches. It will enliven any space and add a touch of whimsy to a formal setting.

Start with a base coat in an eggshell finish. This sheen will take the acrylic craft paint the best. Sketch your branches first; let them grow up naturally, as if rooted in the floor. Then add the leaves, letting them bump up against the wall moldings, as if they were window frames. While the pattern may look random, it has a sense of order. Just like the tree branches growing outside.

Paint: Benjamin Moore's Woodlawn Blue (base coat), and FolkArt's Barn Wood (twigs) and Metallic Pure Gold (leaves)

time Two days
difficulty Easy. Just be sure to practice your strokes on foam board first for the surest line.

tools and materials
See what you need to prep your walls and paint the base coat, starting on page 48.

painter's tape

white blackboard chalk

damp sponge for erasing errant chalk lines

small, round artist's brush

foam board painted the base color so that you can practice your strokes

latex paint in an eggshell finish for the walls

acrylic craft paint in two colors for the twigs and leaves

See how to prep for and paint the **perfect base coat,** page 48.

1

Draw the pattern

> Once the base coat is dry, use painter's tape to create an edge along the bottom, where the branches will start, to give you a clean line.

> Starting at that base line, sketch the branches with chalk, erasing mistakes with a damp sponge. Imagine how a plant would grow up from the ground, and experiment till you get a look you like.

> Establish the structure by sketching all the branches first, then add the leaves.

2

Prepare the paint

> Acrylic craft paint is a good choice for the branches and leaves because it delivers the right color intensity and is available in small quantities. For the branches and leaf outlines, thin 4 parts paint with 1 part water to achieve a soft, semitranslucent line. You want it somewhat sheer so that you don't get a harsh-looking, solid brushstroke.

Tip Try a few different batches of thinned acrylic craft paint to see what formula works best for you. Be sure to jot down your recipe in case you need to mix up more.

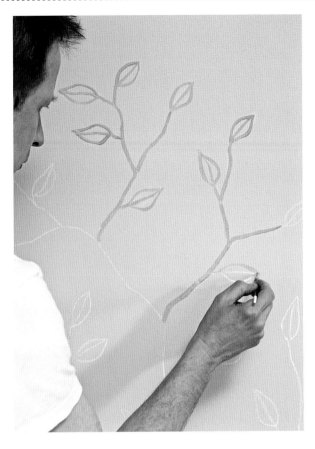

3
Paint the branches

> Practice loading a small, round artist's brush and creating the brown twigs and leaf outlines on painted foam board. Once you're comfortable with your stroke, move to the walls. It's fine to paint right over the chalk lines; you can erase any errant marks later. Let the branches dry thoroughly.

4
Fill in the leaves

> For the leaves, thin 4 parts paint with 1 part water and practice on the foam board first to get the right translucency. When you're comfortable with your stroke, move to the walls. Let dry, then add a second coat; you want the structure of the leaves to show through. This keeps the pattern light and airy, and more natural looking, too.

Oversize floral mural

→ To give your walls a one-of-a-kind look that is more personal than preprinted paper, start sketching. You might want a pattern to follow first, of course. To find one, start small and think big. Anything can be your inspiration—a swatch of fabric, a scarf, even a piece of gift wrap.

All you need is tracing paper, and a level and a chalk line to make a grid; then you can start transferring your design to the wall. Fill it in with latex paint and an artist's brush; a neutral base coat makes the pattern really come alive. Try it in a tiny powder room, where it's easy to take a big risk. Or put it to work in a dining room—it's a good place to be theatrical since you're mostly there in the evening.

time About three days
difficulty Moderate to hard. You need a sure hand and a good eye.

tools and materials
See what you need to prep your walls and paint the base coat, starting on page 48.

tracing paper and **pencil** to copy the pattern

chalk line, pale chalk dust, and **level** to create a grid on the wall

white blackboard chalk to transfer the pattern to the wall

medium, round artist's brush

cut bucket and **liners**

damp sponge to erase chalk lines

latex paint in three colors for the design—plus a neutral color for the base coat

[**ESSENTIAL TOOL**]
CHALK LINE
Creating a grid with a chalk line will make transferring your mural to the wall much easier. Try filling it with baby powder; it will wash off faster when you're done.

Paint: Benjamin Moore's Summer Shower (base coat), Blair Gold (pattern outline), Salisbury Green (pattern interior), and Province Blue (pattern background)

1

Make a pattern

> Using tracing paper and a pencil, borrow a pattern from a book, a scrap of wallpaper, or a swatch of fabric. If the design you like is on an object, like a rug, take a photo, make a photocopy, and enlarge it. Trace the largest shapes, and make the pattern wider than it is tall so that it can wrap around the room without repeating. Draw a grid of 1-inch squares on the traced pattern.

See how to prep for and paint the **perfect base coat,** page 48.

2

Create a grid on the wall

> Once your base coat is dry, use a chalk line, pale chalk dust, and a level to snap horizontal and vertical chalk lines on the walls at regular intervals—here, every 2 feet for a standard 8-foot ceiling.

> Use blackboard chalk to transfer the design— here, it's now 24 times larger—square by square onto the walls. Step back periodically to check that the design connects gracefully.

Tip Another way to get your pattern on the wall is with a video projector. Scan your drawn pattern into your computer, then use the projector to enlarge the drawing to fit one wall; outline the shapes in chalk. Repeat, working your way around the room.

3

Paint the outlines

> Using a round artist's brush and long, smooth strokes, outline the pattern, painting right over the chalk. Let dry. Gently erase any remaining chalk lines, including the grid, with a damp sponge so that they won't distract you during Step 4.

→ **online helper**
Download a template for this design at **thisoldhouse.com/books**

4

Add two softly contrasting shades

> Using the cleaned artist's brush, dab on the paint color that goes around the outlines for the background. As you work, let a bit of the base color show through to add depth; let dry. Repeat the process with the remaining paint color inside the outlines. Both field colors will have a two-dimensional, mottled look, while the pattern's outlines remain crisp.

CHAPTER 3

Woodwork

The interior trim that surrounds doors and windows and runs along walls as baseboard, crown molding, or wainscot actually defines the style of your home. In fact, it adds so much rich detail, it's hard to imagine what a house would look like without it.

Painting these important architectural elements—as well as window sashes, doors, wall paneling, and stair parts—protects them against scuffs and makes them easier to clean. It also highlights their crisp forms, making molding profiles really stand out. The preferred paints for woodwork have a glossy sheen that makes them tough but also shows off every surface imperfection. So when it comes to trimwork, meticulous prep and careful brushwork are more critical than ever.

Paint: Olympic's River Reed (walls), Weeping Willow (wainscot), and Delicate White (trim)

prep basics

Prep your woodwork

→ Preparing wood trim takes time—much more time than it takes to actually apply the paint— but as any pro will tell you, every minute you spend before you pick up a brush pays dividends when you lay down that first coat.

Here's what you need to know to prep your trim, whether you're starting from scratch with bare wood or getting previously painted or stained woodwork ready for a fresh coat.

tools and materials

putty knife or **painter's 5-in-1 tool**

wood filler Select either lightweight spackling, powdered water putty, a two-part mix, or wood epoxy.

damp washcloth and **clothing iron**

silicone-carbide sandpaper in 80, 100, 120, 150, and 220 grit

pull-type paint scraper

wet-dry vacuum with brush attachment

tack cloth or **reusable microfiber cloth**

paintbrushes sized for the surface you're priming. Select natural bristles for oil-based primers, nylon-polyester for water-based.

coarse- and **fine-grit sanding sponges**

all-purpose primer-sealer either oil-based or latex

paintable caulk and **caulk gun**

FOR UNFINISHED WOOD

1 **Fill nail holes.** Paint won't hide these holes, no matter how small they are; applying wood filler with a flexible putty knife is a necessary first step. When using premixed spackling, overfill the hole slightly to allow for shrinkage. With powdered water putty or a two-part mix, neither of which shrinks, smooth them flush with the surface.

2 **Remove dents.** You can get rid of errant hammer blows and other dents with a targeted application of steam. Wet the dent completely, then cover it with a damp terry washcloth and apply a hot iron to the cloth for several seconds. The heat and moisture will make the wood fibers expand, and the dent should disappear.

3 **Sand.** A thorough sanding removes dirt, scratches, and excess filler. Start with 80-grit sandpaper and move to 120 grit, then finish with 150.

4 **Dust.** Sanding generates dust, which can interfere with paint's adhesion and make it rough and unsightly. Getting rid of it requires two steps.

> Use a vacuum with a brush attachment to suck up most of the sanding residue.

> Follow up by wiping

WARNING:
If your house was built before the 1978 lead-paint ban, have the paint tested before you scrape or sand it. The EPA's website, epa.gov/lead, has guidelines for testing and removal.

no detectable bump at the boundary between wood and paint. Finish sanding with 150-grit sandpaper.

4 **Dust.** Get rid of all sanding dust (see Step 4 for unfinished wood). Finish with a tack cloth or a reusable microfiber cloth.

5 **Prime.** If the existing paint surface is in good condition, with no fillers or exposed wood, and you know what kind of paint it is (oil-based or water-based), you can skip the priming step and simply apply a compatible top coat. (Latex paint works over both oil and latex paints. Oil paint should only be applied over oil.) Otherwise, apply a coat or two of primer before the top coat.

FOR STAINED, CLEAR-FINISHED WOOD

Follow Steps 1 to 5 for painted wood. Note: Since clear finishes do not contain lead, you don't have to worry if it's necessary to scrape or sand. Use only an oil-based primer to prevent natural wood pigments from bleeding through.

Tip To get into woodwork crevices, use a flexible foam sanding sponge. If you are preparing a flat surface, use sandpaper. To make a half sheet last, fold it in thirds so that the grit-coated faces don't touch.

everything down with a sticky tack cloth (cheesecloth impregnated with beeswax) or a reusable microfiber cloth.

5 **Prime.** A primer is formulated to do three things: adhere well to bare wood, seal the wood so that the top coat will have a uniform sheen, and provide a surface that the top coat will stick to nicely.

> Fast-drying primers will let you apply the top coat sooner, but they don't level out as well as slow-drying ones. For the smoothest finish, apply two coats of primer, then sand with 220-grit sandpaper until perfectly smooth.

6 **Caulk.** Cover any open cracks or seams between trim and wall, or between pieces of trim, with a paintable caulk. Smooth the

bead with a wet finger or the back of a clean spoon.

FOR PAINTED WOOD

1 **Scrape.** Look for loose or bubbled paint or drips left by previous painters. Gently remove them with a pull-type paint scraper or a 5-in-1 tool, taking care not to gouge the underlying wood.

2 **Repair damage.** Surface imperfections will echo through the new paint, so take care to remove them before you start painting. Cover nail holes, scratches, and dents with wood filler (see Steps 1 and 2 for unfinished wood). Fill deep cracks with epoxy thickened with wood sanding dust.

3 **Sand.** Smooth the surface with 100-grit sandpaper. Pay close attention to the edges of any spots where bare wood shows through; there should be

ALTERNATE TECHNIQUE:
STRIPPING OLD PAINT

In the life of every painted surface, there eventually comes a time when all that paint has to go. It may be so thick that it obscures the details of the wood underneath. It may be poorly adhered and chipping off. Or, worst of all, it may be loaded with lead and therefore a potential health hazard. Whatever the reason, stripping should not be undertaken lightly. It's a slow, messy process. But once you're done, you'll have a pristine surface that will look fantastic when you give it a fresh coat.

→

tools and materials

solvent-resistant tape or **heat-resistant aluminum-foil tape** to mask off areas you don't want to strip

plastic bucket to put the stripped paint in

6-mil plastic sheeting

chip brush for applying chemical strippers

gloves Neoprene and butyl offer good protection if you're stripping with chemicals. If you're using a heat gun, leather gloves will insulate your hands from the heat.

long-sleeve shirt and **goggles** to protect yourself from accidental chemical splashes

respirator with organic cartridges to keep you from breathing paint dust or chemical fumes

plastic push-type scrapers These are gentle on wood but shouldn't be used with heat

[1]. Try pottery scrapers for hard-to-reach spots [2].

metal pull scrapers Look for ones with contoured blades to fit molding profiles [3].

dental picks A set of these is handy for getting paint out of crevices [4].

sanding cord Use it to clean crevices on balusters or spindles [5]. For a lighter touch, try twine.

brass brush Gently scrubs away softened paint and does

not react with chemical strippers [6].

nylon scouring pads These take stubborn residue off flat and curved surfaces. Also good for smoothing stripped wood [7]. Do not use steel wool.

chemical stripper, heat gun, or **infrared heater** See "Pick your chemical stripper" (opposite), or use one of these plug-in devices for heat stripping.

PREPPING TO STRIP

1_ Tape. Mask off areas you don't want stripped. Use solvent-resistant tape if applying chemical strippers, aluminum-foil tape if using heat.

2_ Cover the floor. Tape down the edges of 6-mil plastic sheeting at least 6 feet beyond your work area.

3_ Protect yourself. Don gloves, a long-sleeve shirt, goggles, and a respirator.

TIPS FOR CHEMICAL STRIPPING

These chemicals work by dissolving the resins in paint. The strength of the stripper and the stubbornness of the finish determine stripping speed.

1_ Consider consistency. In most cases, choose a thick semipaste, which will cling to vertical surfaces. Thinner strippers are best for removing the residues left after most of the paint has come off.

2_ Brush on a thick layer. The more you can apply, the longer it will remain active on the paint.

3_ Leave it be. Once applied, stripper should not be disturbed. Let it skin over and trap its active ingredients next to the paint. Covering the stripper with a layer of plastic wrap will keep it working longer.

4_ Don't rush. Wait until the stripper does its job before starting to scrape.

5_ Clean up. This final step removes any residue that might interfere with the new paint. Follow the directions on the stripper's label.

TIPS FOR HEAT STRIPPING

Not as messy or slow as chemical stripping, heat stripping is also fairly safe, as long as you stay focused. With lead-based paint, the heat gun temperature should never exceed 1100 degrees F. (Paint softens at about 400 degrees F.) We recommend using either a temperature-adjustable heat gun or an infrared heater.

1_ Mask with foil or foil tape. Aluminum reflects the heat away from surfaces you don't want stripped.

2_ Keep moving. Holding the heat in one place for too long can burn the paint, char the wood, or even start a fire. Experiment until you find just how far you need to hold the gun from the paint so that it bubbles up but doesn't blacken.

3_ Keep a metal roller pan nearby. It makes a handy place to set down a hot gun or heater.

4_ Finish with chemicals. It's hard to remove every bit of paint just with heat. A final application of a chemical stripper should get rid of all those residual bits.

Pick your chemical stripper

Most paint stores and home centers stock dozens of liquid and paste chemical strippers. Basically, there are two things you need to know:
> All of them will eat through almost any finish.
> Generally, the safer the stripper is, the slower it works.
With that in mind, here's a rundown of the three basic categories.

Fast

Most strippers in this category contain methylene chloride, also called dichloromethane (DCM). This aggressive chemical quickly softens almost any paint or finish. It is not flammable. However, in addition to being a possible carcinogen, it can cause skin and lung irritation and a host of other potential health problems. Like carbon monoxide, it reduces the amount of oxygen in the blood when inhaled, which can mean a trip to the ER. Stripped wood must be cleaned with alcohol to remove residue.

Fast-working strippers without DCM typically use acetone, methanol, and toluene (AMT), a mixture that is very volatile, highly flammable, and also dangerous to breathe. On the plus side, this stripper leaves a paint-ready surface.

If you're going to use these fast strippers, a respirator, goggles, and gloves are essential. To be even safer, move the work outdoors.

Try: *Klean-Strip, Zar, Rock Miracle, Star 10*

Medium

These strippers typically contain N-methyl-2-pyrrolidone (NMP), which isn't flammable like AMT or as toxic or volatile as methylene chloride. But you'll still need to wear gloves and goggles, and keep the work area well ventilated. To strip multiple layers, you may need to apply a second coat and let it sit overnight. Wood cleanup requires water or denatured alcohol.

Try: *Citristrip, Back to Nature, Peel Away 7*

Slow

These nonflammable strippers use dibasic esters (DBE), sodium hydroxide (caustic soda), or other nontoxic ingredients. This type can be used indoors without special ventilation or a respirator, but gloves and goggles are still a must. The downside is that these strippers may take 12 hours or more to work and, because they're water-based, can raise the grain and loosen veneers. Use detergent and water to clean wood stripped with DBE. Caustics require a vinegar treatment follow-up before wood can be painted; test first to make sure it has a neutral pH.

Try: *Safest Stripper, Peel Away 1, RemovAll*

○ TRIM TECHNIQUES

The glossier the paint, the more demanding the application. Start with the moldings nearest the ceiling and work down, keeping these priorities in mind with each one

Before you start, cover any surfaces you don't want painted with tape and a drop cloth.

> **Crown molding.** Start in a corner. Right-handers generally work to the right as they move around a room; left-handers go to the left.

> **Window casing.** First, paint the edge of a side casing where it meets the wall, then its stop (the vertical piece that holds the sash in the window). Finish by painting the casing's flat face. Repeat this sequence—outside edge, inside stop, face—for the head and the other side casing. If the sides are flush with the top piece (the head casing), start at the bottom of a side casing and paint its face up to the joint with the head casing. If the joints are not flush, paint the head casing first, then brush the side casings from the top down. When the casing is done, paint the bottom apron, then the stool, or windowsill.

> **Door casing.** As with window casing, paint the outside and inside edges before painting each face. If the head casing is flush with the sides, brush the face from the bottom up to the head casing and continue around the opening. If the head casing isn't flush with the sides, paint it first, then brush the faces of the side casings from the top down.

> **Chair rail.** As with crown, start in a corner and work your way around the room.

> **Baseboard.** This trim typically has three parts: a profiled cap, a flat board in the middle, and a shoe molding against the floor. Starting in a corner, paint just the cap and the shoe first, as far as you can reach, then go back and paint the face in between. Always back-brush into the wet edge as you start a new section.

> **Staircase trim.** Working from the top down, paint the stringers first, using the same technique as for baseboards, then paint the risers. Use a narrow brush to paint the balusters. Cover each one entirely, and before moving to the next, inspect every side for drips. Finally, paint the newel posts from the top down.

Application tips

Whatever trim you're working on, these techniques ensure a uniform, no-drip coat of color.

Use the light. Whenever possible, work away from a window. The light reflecting off the wet paint will help you to easily see any missed spots or drips.

Land in a dry spot. Always place a fully loaded brush in a dry spot, ahead of the wet edge, then brush back into the wet edge before continuing.

Spread, then tip. Distribute each brushload of paint evenly over the surface, then lightly drag just the tips of the brush over the wet paint to level out any brushmarks.

Work with the grain. Stroke the brush in line with the trim's length.

Start away from inside corners. Avoid the temptation to brush into them. Instead, place the loaded brush a couple of inches from the corner and, with the brush handle pointing away from the corner, make a series of quick outward strokes as you back in toward the corner.

Brush off outside corners. A careless painter runs a brush over the corner, scraping wet paint off the bristles and causing ugly drips. Use this technique instead: Pull the brush off the end of the molding like it's an airplane taking off from an aircraft carrier. Done correctly, there won't be any drips.

Idea file

SIX INSPIRING WAYS
TO MAKE TRIMWORK
STAND OUT WITH COLOR

Extra dimension
A two-color
scheme gives this
newel post and stair
wall added depth,
while the chestnut-
brown cap and
handrail provide
definition.
Paint: Olympic's
Delicate White and
Weeping Willow

Tone on tone
Gray-painted woodwork creates a
subtle color play with creamy white walls
and a taupe bench. Glidden's Silvery
Moonlight (trim), Caroline Strand (wall),
and Petal Pink (bench)

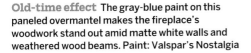

Old-time effect The gray-blue paint on this
paneled overmantel makes the fireplace's
woodwork stand out amid matte white walls and
weathered wood beams. Paint: Valspar's Nostalgia

Closely related A classic balustrade gets a modern sensibility with paint colors just steps away from each other in the yellow-green to blue-green range, and an all-white backdrop. Paint: Valspar's Tangy Dill, Spring Lawn, Can't Miss Lime, Jaunty Green, Sassy Green, Salamander, Lovely Green, Green Sea, Cool Rain, Ocean Soul, Sea Swell, Starry Sky, Green Suede, Southern Garden, and La Fonda Turquoise (balusters), and Clean White (walls, stairs)

Well connected Painting the risers and baseboard the same color as the adjacent door and casing helps unify the stairs with the room where they land. Paint: Glidden's Skipping Stone (doors, casing) and Pearl Essence White (walls)

Accent borders Contrasting ribbons of paint strengthen the fireplace's role as focal point and reinforce the room's color scheme. Paint: Pratt & Lambert's Raffia Tan (walls, border), Red Rhythm (trim), and Designer White (mantel)

○WINDOW SASH TECHNIQUES

Toss the painter's tape. With a 2-inch angled brush, a putty knife, and a razor blade, you can get a clean paint job on any window sash. Just follow these steps for double-hung windows, the most challenging type to paint

1_ Top sash. Raise the bottom sash and lower the top sash until they've almost switched places. Paint the exposed parts of the top sash (now on the bottom), including any muntins (the cross pieces). Overlap the paint slightly onto the glass.

> Reverse the sashes' positions, without fully closing them, and finish painting the top one's stiles and rails.

2_ Bottom sash. Paint the entire bottom sash: muntins first, if there are any, then rails, followed by the stiles. When painting stiles, take care not to lap paint onto the stops, the vertical pieces that hold the sash in the window.

3_Slide sashes up and down. As soon as the paint is dry to the touch, slide each sash up and down. This will break the bond of any paint that may have seeped between the stops and the stiles.

4_ Clean the glass. When the paint is dry, place the edge of a wide putty knife on the glass, tight against the wood. With a razor blade, scrape up to the knife, peeling paint off the glass. Continue around the perimeter of each pane. You will be left with neat paint lines that seal the seam between wood and glass and prevent condensation from reaching the wood.

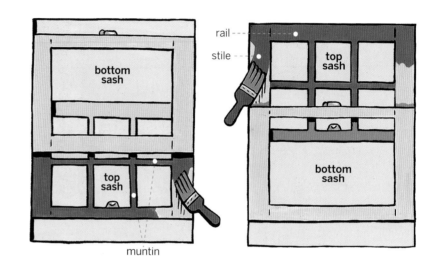

muntin

pro advice TOM SILVA, TOH GENERAL CONTRACTOR

"Be careful to not let paint get between the sash and the stop or you might glue the window shut."

wet paint

dry paint

Idea file

FIVE PAINT SCHEMES
FOR WINDOWS, FROM SUBTLE
TO STRIKING

Paint it black
The windows in this vintage-look
kitchen were painted glossy black
to echo the floor stain. The contrast
they provide helps ground the
gleaming white tile walls. Paint:
Sherwin-Williams' Black of Night

Frame the view
Painting stiles, rails,
and muntins a slightly
bolder shade than the
window trim and walls
draws the eye outside
and gives a room added
depth and personality.
Paint: Olympic's Caruso
(windows), Dewmist
Delight (trim, walls), and
By the Sea (daybed)

123

Attention getter
Color can accentuate a special architectural element.
This window wall becomes a dramatic focal point when painted green.
Pale blue outlining the windows and coating the French doors adds
another subtle layer of color. Paint: Glidden's Tahiti (window wall),
Java Sea (window, doors), and Glacier White (walls, ceiling)

Graphic gridwork
Windows don't have to be ceiling high to gain presence from a rich trim color like this charcoal. But here it gives the wall-to-wall panes the look of translucent paneling. Paint: Pratt & Lambert's Café Gray (windows) and Balsa (ceiling)

Pretty as a picture
Bright gold emphasizes the natural light coming through this over-the-sink window, turning it into a framed work of art. Paint: Behr's Marigold

○DOOR TECHNIQUES

Because a paneled door has so many parts, there's a risk of creating lap marks where fresh paint overlaps paint applied earlier that has started to dry. To avoid them, paint the parts in the sequence shown

1_ Moldings. Paint only the profiled edge around one panel. Pull the brush away from corners to avoid leaving puddles. Wipe off any paint that spreads onto a rail or stile.

2_ Panel. As soon as you finish the molding around a panel, paint that panel. Cut in around its perimeter, then fill in the center using vertical strokes. Finally, tip off the entire panel with a series of vertical strokes. Repeat Steps 1 and 2 for all the remaining panels. If they are separated by a center stile, paint it next using the technique in Step 3, but tip off vertically.

3_ Top and middle rails. As you paint rails, don't let the brush touch the molding or scrape against its corners. Carry the paint a bit past the joints where stiles and rails meet. You'll smooth out this overlap when you coat the stiles. Always tip off rails with horizontal strokes.

4_ Stiles. Start at the top. Run the brush along both rail-stile joints to smooth out overlapping paint. To avoid drips, pull the brush gently off the ends. Switch back and forth between stiles so that both leading edges stay wet. As you near the bottom rail, paint it before you finish painting the stiles. Always tip off stiles with vertical strokes.

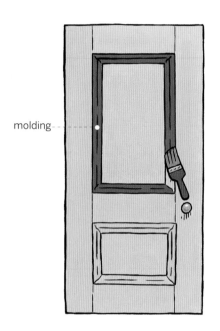

molding

panel

stile

rail

wet paint

dry paint

Idea file
FOUR EASY, UNEXPECTED COLOR IDEAS FOR INTERIOR DOORS

Half and half
Got a room interrupted by a few too many doorways? Try revising its architecture by wrapping it in two contrasting shades. Here, a clean sweep of white—over walls, trim, and door—creates a faux wainscot. Above, a rich marine blue makes wall art pop. Paint: Olympic's King Triton (above) and Delicate White (below)

Focal-point color
Think of a beautiful paneled door as an opportunity for a statement shade. Here a bold citrine livens up the dining area side, with just a hint of the persimmon that brightens the adjacent space. Paint: Pratt & Lambert's Leaf Sprout (front) and Scarlet O'Hara (back)

Well blended
To let a dramatic tub surround take center stage, this entire bath, door included, was cloaked in a singular deep blue hue. Paint: Pratt & Lambert's Anchor's Aweigh

Soft but striking
The pale gray-blue on this attic door and rustic stair railing looks sophisticated instead of sweet, thanks in part to all the black accents around it. Paint: Ralph Lauren Paint's Cloud Blue

WHILE YOU'RE AT IT:
RESTORE YOUR HARDWARE

Good painters remove or cover door hardware first. The other type just slops the brush over any exposed metal. Fortunately, any metal knob, escutcheon plate, or hinge can easily be made to shine again without noxious chemicals. All you need is a slow-cooker and a few simple tools. Here's how to do it:

1_ Cut the paint. Protect the surrounding paint from damage by carefully scoring the perimeter of each escutcheon plate or hinge with a utility knife. Loosen the set screw holding the knob to its spindle and slide out the pieces.

2_ Remove the plates. Gently carve out the paint in the screw slots with the point of the knife. Back out the screws, taking care not to apply a lot of pressure; you don't want the screwdriver to slip and gouge the metal. Once the screws are out, pry off escutcheons and hinges.

3_ Heat and soak. Place the hardware in a slow-cooker with a disposable liner. Cover with water, add a couple of tablespoons of liquid laundry detergent, and turn the heat to MEDIUM. Put on the lid and let everything cook overnight. The next day, remove the hot hardware with tongs.

4_ Scrub. Immediately push off any softened paint with a toothbrush or nylon bristle brush. (A wire brush can scratch.) Paint hardens quickly once out of the pot, so loosen any remaining particles by dipping the pieces back in the hot water.

5_ Wax. Protect the metal with a coat of beeswax polish, rubbed on with a soft cloth. (You can spray on a lacquer finish instead, but if it ever chips or wears off, the metal will have to be chemically stripped.)

6_ Finish. Once your paint job is dry, reinstall your hardware.

○ BEADBOARD TECHNIQUES

Beaded boards come as tongue-and-groove wood strips, sheets of grooved pine, or medium-density fiberboard (MDF). Here are some prep and painting tips to give any kind of beadboard a smooth finish

> **Forget caulk between individual boards.** No amount of caulking on vertical joints is going to prevent the boards from moving as the humidity changes. Besides, when caulk fails, the results aren't pretty or easy to clean up.

> **But always caulk at the base.** Fill the small gaps at the bottom edge of any beadboard wainscot where it's covered by the baseboard cap. Otherwise, they'll become clogged with grime. Smooth the bead of caulk by holding a putty knife vertically and following the contours of the beadboard.

> **Break the bond.** Where old paint is cracked or makes a bridge between individual boards, rake the gap clean with a putty knife and sand the ragged edges before painting.

> **Paint the tongues.** If you can, apply the finish color to the tongue of each board before you install it. That way, if a joint opens up, there won't be a color contrast to highlight the gap.

> **Brush individual boards one at a time.** This reduces the chance for paint to flow into a joint and cling to two different boards as it dries. If the paint does bridge a joint, clean it out before it dries.

Idea file

FOUR STANDOUT PAINT APPROACHES FOR BEADBOARD PANELING

White on white
This living room's double-bead paneling is painted the same warm white as the rest of the woodwork, making the trim details really stand out. The result: a simple cottage look. Paint: Glidden's Stowe White

Country update
Bright red chairs give
a breakfast nook with
blue-gray wainscot a
crisp, unfussy look.
Paint: Glidden's Island
View (wainscot) and
Victorian Red (chairs)

Spring greens
Pure white bathroom fixtures soften a
dramatic pairing of warm yellowish green
on the tub surround and wainscot, and
cool greenish yellow on the walls. Paints:
Pratt & Lambert's Fairway Green
(wainscot) and Queen's Lace (walls)

Airy overhead
A beadboard ceiling warms up a vintage-look
bath. Try a two-person approach when painting
on high: one person to roll the boards while
another brushes the beads. Paint: Pratt &
Lambert's Designer White (wainscot, ceiling)
and Luminous Cloud (walls)

CHAPTER 4

Cabinets, built-ins, & furniture

These pieces get plenty of hard use in a household. Juice and gravy are spilled down cabinet fronts. Hardcovers and CDs are scraped on and off bookshelves. Chairs and tables get banged and bumped. Whatever the battle scar or bruise brought about by daily living, a fresh coat of paint can make it disappear and provide a new hard-wearing—and easy to clean— surface for built-in cabinets and freestanding furniture pieces. And it does all that while adding a hearty dose of eye-pleasing color to your surroundings.

Paint: Pratt & Lambert's Castilian Gold (cabinets) and Indigo (island), and C2 Paint's Sisal (walls) and Cheetah (trim)

Prep all surfaces

→ Achieving a nice, glossy painted finish on cabinets, built-ins, or furniture depends, as with any paint job, on the quality of your prep work. Before bristles ever brush against wood, a lot of time has to be devoted to getting the surface ready to accept paint. That means properly cleaning, sanding, and priming every inch, or the finish color won't stick well.

The steps shown here, demonstrated on kitchen cabinets, will cover the basics for any built-in or furniture piece.

tools and materials

rosin paper to cover and protect floor and countertops

4-mil plastic sheeting to protect the backsplash and surrounding walls from drips and splatters

painter's tape for masking

screwdriver or **drill/driver** to remove doors and hardware

sponges to clean surfaces

degreaser or **TSP substitute** to remove dirt and oily residue

water putty or **two-part wood filler** for old hardware holes

putty knife to spread filler

100-grit and **220-grit silicone-carbide sandpaper**

fine- and **medium-grit sanding sponges** Use the fine-grit to smooth profiled trim.

random-orbit sander (optional) for faster sanding of flat areas

wet-dry vacuum with brush attachment

reusable microfiber cloths to remove sanding dust between coats

cup hooks and **clothesline** for hanging the doors while they dry

2½-inch angled nylon-polyester paintbrush

oil-based or **latex primer-sealer** to create a clean, smooth surface for the paint. Look for ones labeled "high build" and "sandable." If, however, cabinets are faced with laminate, select a primer suited for glossy surfaces.

prep basics

1 Prep the area. Mask off adjacent walls and overlay floors with rosin paper held in place with painter's tape. Cover any backsplash with 4-mil plastic. Take out cabinet shelves and label them so that you know where they came from.

2 Label hardware. Remove all pulls and knobs, and unscrew all hinges and doors. Pull out drawers and, if possible, unscrew the fronts. Flag each piece and its corresponding opening with matching, numbered pieces of tape; store hardware from each part in separate, zippered plastic bags.

3 Clean. Paint won't adhere properly to any surface coated with even the thinnest layer of oil. Wipe down every inch with a

sponge and a degreaser, such as a TSP substitute. Repeat with a clean sponge. Avoid any cleaner containing ammonia; there's no effective way to neutralize it, and it will cause oil-based paint to yellow.

4 Fill. Using a putty knife, fill any dings, divots, and dents with a no-shrink, two-part wood filler or water putty. If you're changing out the knobs and pulls, fill the old hardware holes, too. This type of filler turns rock-hard when it sets; take off the excess as you go, to save sanding time later.

5 Sand. Smooth the filled spots and rough up the old finish with 100-grit sandpaper and a medium-grit sanding sponge. Sand with the grain until the entire surface is dull, taking care not to round over the edges.

6 Dust. Vacuum up the dust, then capture any remaining particles by wiping the surface with a reusable microfiber cloth. Repeat with a clean cloth.

7 Prepare for hanging. Screw a pair of cup hooks into each door and drawer front so that you can hang them up to dry. Put the screws into the top edge of upper-cabinet doors and

into the bottom edges of drawers and lower-cabinet doors spaced about a foot apart. String two parallel lengths of clothesline about a foot apart and make them taut.

8 Prime. Lay the drawer fronts and doors facedown, and brush on a coat of primer using a 2½-inch brush. Coat the interior panel first, then the rails and stiles. Leave the doors horizontal so that the paint will level off.

> While the doors are drying, prime the inside of the cabinet boxes, if desired, then the outside.

> When the drawer fronts and doors are dry to the touch, flip them over and paint the other side. After that side is dry enough to handle, hang them from the clotheslines.

9 Sand. Allow the primer to dry, as indicated on the label. Smooth away any brushstrokes using 220-grit sandpaper; smooth profiles and other grooves with a fine-grit sanding sponge. Sand the cabinet boxes and frames in the same manner.

10 Dust again. Vacuum all surfaces thoroughly, then wipe them down with a reusable microfiber cloth. If necessary, apply a second coat of primer and resand the surface to achieve a smooth base coat. Remove the dust before applying the finish coat.

Tip To make the open pores in woods like oak or walnut disappear, coat the wood with a paste filler, such as Pore-O-Pac, or a high-build, brush-on primer, like Brushing Putty.

brush
basics

Cabinet painting 101

→ Once the tedious prep work is done, it's time for the fun part: applying the paint. Whether you're painting kitchen or bathroom cabinets, built-in bookcases, or flea-market furniture, you want to work from the top down and from the inside edges to the outside ones.

You will be living close to these surfaces for years to come, so don't shrink from buying the best brushes and paints that you can afford. And consider this project your master class in painting technique—no shortcuts, drips, or "holidays" (missed spots) allowed.

tools and materials

3-inch angled paintbrush Choose one with natural bristles for oil or one with nylon-polyester bristles for latex.

220-grit silicone-carbide sandpaper to sand surfaces smooth

fine-grit sanding sponge to smooth profiled trim

random-orbit sander (optional) for faster sanding of flat areas

wet-dry vacuum with brush attachment

reusable microfiber cloths to remove sanding dust between coats

oil-based paint or **100 percent acrylic latex paint specially formulated for cabinetry or high-traffic areas** You will need about a gallon per coat on a bank of four upper and lower cabinets.

1 Brush on the top coats.
Break out a new brush to put down the top coat. Beginning on the backs of the drawer fronts and doors, brush on the paint in thin coats, going with the grain. Paint the panels first, then work your way out to the rails and stiles.

> Distribute the paint evenly: Brush in the same direction as the wood grain using long, parallel strokes. Don't let paint accumulate in corners, where it can run and drip. With latex, you have only two or three strokes before it starts to dry and drag. Oil-based paint is more forgiving of repeated brushing.

> Tip off. As soon the paint is distributed, hold the brush nearly upright and gently drag the bristles' soft tips over the surface of the wet paint in one direction. This step erases brush marks and sets the stage for even drying.

> While the doors and drawers are drying, keep them perfectly flat to allow the paint to level out. Meanwhile, paint the cabinet boxes and face frames.

> Once the doors and drawer fronts are dry to the touch, flip them over and coat the faces, again working from the interior panel out to the rails and stiles. Remember to tip off each section you paint while it's still wet, to smooth brush marks.

Paint: Benjamin
Moore's Candy Green

ALTERNATE TECHNIQUE:
SPRAY ON THE PAINT

> For a fast, factory-quality finish, you can't beat a paint sprayer. But proper preparation and technique are key.

> Follow the prep steps on page 134. Good technique means pulling the paint-gun trigger before your gun is pointed at the surface you're painting, letting go only when it's past the work, and always holding the gun from the same distance—too close and you'll cause drips, too far away and you'll waste paint. Spray edges first, then fill in the field, making sure each pass overlaps the previous one by about 50 percent.

> Spray painting is more demanding than brushing. You'll need to be exacting in how you thin the paint before you start and how you clean up after you're done. And because there's lots of overspray, wear a respirator and carefully mask off and cover every interior surface that you don't want paint to land on. Work outside, if possible, on doors and drawer fronts.

Tip Check the weather. Extreme temperatures and humidity can affect paint setup time. To help paint level out, mix in a small amount of compatible paint conditioner.

2 > **Leave it alone.** Disturbing paint after tip off gets you the opposite of smooth. Let doors and drawer fronts sit flat until they're dry to the touch. Then hang them from the clotheslines to fully dry before applying the second coat.

3 **Repeat.** Sand everything with 220-grit sandpaper, going with the grain. Vacuum and wipe down every surface to remove dust, then apply the second coat, as in Step 1. When the paint is dry, mount the hardware and reinstall the drawers and doors.

Oil, latex, or a combo of both

The first question many homeowners ask: Should they paint their cabinets with oil or latex? Latex often gets the nod as more environmentally and user-friendly because it cleans up with water and has a low odor. But many pros still favor oil for its harder, smoother, more durable film. Relatively new and not yet widely available is a third type of paint, known as oil modified, which combines the attributes of an oil finish with the low VOCs and easy cleanup of a latex. Bottom line: Any of these paints will provide a good finish, as long as it has a high percentage of titanium-dioxide pigment and uses high-quality resins. These ingredients are costly, so be skeptical of products sold for low prices. If you go with latex paint, make sure it's a 100 percent acrylic formulation, which offers greater durability and adhesion than cheaper vinyl acrylics.

IDEA FILE:
KITCHEN CABINETS

Whether you choose a color that matches your walls or go for drama with a contrasting shade, painting your cabinets is the quickest, most cost-effective way to renovate your kitchen

Light and airy
An ultra-pale shade of dusty blue highlights this kitchen's detailed panels and range mantel, making the room feel more like a soothing sanctuary than a busy family hub. Paint: Ralph Lauren Paint's Lisbon Blue (cabinets) and Weathered Stone (wall)

Sophisticated mix
The key to multiple hues coexisting so peacefully in this space? The largest field of color—on cabinets and built-ins—is subdued. A small blue island and even smaller red table define the work and eating areas. Yellow trim on the cabinet doors provides a cheery accent. Paint: Olympic's Frosty Pine (cabinets), Del Sol (cabinet trim), Blue Oasis (island), and Red Gumball (table)

Bold and bright
Unexpectedly vivid yellow paint puts a lemony twist on otherwise traditional flat-panel cabinets. The workhorse island grounds the space in a more subdued gray-green. Paint: Farrow & Ball's Citron (perimeter cabinets) and Chappell Green (island)

Opposites attract
A floor-to-ceiling coat of bright lime brings factory-style metal cabinetry into the modern age. (Just be sure to use a primer for metal before painting.) Window sashes painted red—green's complement—reinforce the playful palette even more. Paint: Sherwin-Williams' Lime Rickey (cabinets), Poinsettia (windows), and Extra White (walls)

Vintage flair
Geometric chinoiserie trim gets its due in attention-grabbing cherry red, which pops against crisp white cabinets. Yellow walls make for a warm background that also ties in with the checkerboard floor. Paint: Benjamin Moore's Atrium White (cabinets), Strawberry Red (cabinet trim), and Amarillo (walls)

Eye-catching color

Vintage-style woodwork details really stand out when painted in glowing shades of yellow and green. Red adds depth to the interiors of open-front cabinets for a dramatic display. Paint: Behr's Geranium Leaf (cabinets, trim), Ruby Ring (cabinet interiors), and Daffodil Yellow (walls)

Natural beauty
Cabinet boxes painted in earthy shades of pale green and blue break
up an expanse of orange-toned wood while complementing its warm grain.
Paint: Glidden's Misty Glen (above) and Coastal Blue (below)

○ IDEA FILE:
BUILT-INS

We love built-ins for their ability to lend a home character and extra storage. But they also offer a great opportunity to pump up a house's palette and give plain walls extra dimension

Restful beds
Glossy white paint ensures that the simple platform bunkbeds in this nautical-themed children's room pop against a sea of light-blue paneled walls. Paint: Behr's Ultra Pure White (built-in beds, ceiling) and Madras Blue (walls)

Cozy cubby
Tucked in a stairwell landing and painted the same muted green as the surrounding walls, this open-front closet becomes a convenient, inconspicuous spot for outdoor essentials. Paint: Behr's Rocky Mountain Sky (built-in)

Elegantly framed
The white paint that coats the built-in in this smartly appointed office
creates a crisp boundary for the russet-colored paneling that lines its back.
Paint: Sherwin-Williams' Pure White (built-in) and Spicy Hue (back)

Architectural flair
Repeating this two-tone wainscot's painted batten details on the front of the window seat helps it blend in *and* stand out. Paint: Farrow & Ball's Fawn (lower wall), James White (trim), and Slipper Satin (upper wall)

Savvy silhouette
Enlarge a small space by painting built-ins to match the walls. Then add a color contrast to details like this hutch's open back and latticework design to make them pop. Paint: Ralph Lauren Paint's Artist's Studio (built-in, wall), Lifevest Orange (back), and Tackroom White (detail)

Custom look
Turn stock cabinets into an architectural statement by building them in, using trim to tie them together, and painting them a catchy accent color. Paint: Pratt & Lambert's Malaga (built-ins), Silver Lining (window trim, ceiling), and Chalk Grey (wall)

Wake-up call

The inherent drama of this breakfast nook's high-back bench is multiplied tenfold when painted an unexpected yellow-green and paired with brilliant blue chairs. Paint: Sherwin-Williams' Escapade Gold (bench) and Jay Blue (chairs)

Sunny delight

The classic combo of red and yellow reaches new heights in this cheerful mudroom. The key is balancing the intensity of color—bright red paneling is softened by cabinetry in a mellower shade of yellow. Paint: Olympic's Pale Moss Green(cabinetry), Del Sol (cabinet trim), and Red Gumball (paneling)

Back to black
Ebony bookshelves deliver depth to a surround of plain white walls.
Pumpkin-colored furnishings warm up what could have been a stark contrast.
Paint: Sherman-Williams' Bohemian Black (built-ins) and Pure White (walls)

○ IDEA FILE:
FURNITURE

There's no better way to wake up tired chairs, tables, and dressers than with a few artfully applied coats of color

Kicked-up console
It may rest upon formal turned legs, but this behind-the-sofa table is anything but stuffy, thanks to bold stripes in various widths and colors stretching across its top. Paint: Sherwin-Williams' Capri, Extra White, Reticence, Black Magic, Ravishing Coral, Mocha, Sassy Green, and Ramie

Variations on a theme
This shapely bureau gets even more gussied up with drawers painted varying dusky shades and lavender. The result has an elegant ombré effect. Paint: Ralph Lauren Paint's Weathered Stone (bureau, two drawers), Lamp Room Grey (two drawers), Duchess Lilac (one drawer, wall), and Tackroom White (dresser)

Red-hot seats These Windsor-inspired dining chairs get a leg up on similar styles thanks to a glossy coat of rouge enamel on their bottom half. When painting details such as these seats' spindles, avoid drips by working the brush in a side-to-side motion. Paint: Valspar's Clean White (chairs) and Passion Pink (legs)

Scandinavian style
Folksy white stencils—inspired by a favorite sweater—echo the gracefully curving lines of this stacked armoire, painted denim blue with just a hint of cerulean trim. Paint: C2 Paint's Proxy (armoire), Electric (trim), and Architectural White (stencils)

Panels with panache
Indulge in a little pattern play by covering an already bold room divider with a repeating motif in a contrasting color. All you need is a stencil and some imagination. Paint: Olympic's Spiced Butternut (room divider), Teaberry Blossom (stencil), and Ship's Harbor (wall)

Wonderfully weathered
It may be brand new, but this bureau boasts the charm of a beloved antique. To get a similar distressed effect, layer moss-green paint over a base coat of light blue, then gently wipe a bit of the green away before it has dried. Stencil the numbers on top, then sand down to the base coat when the cream-colored paint is dry. Paint: California Paints' Robin's Egg (bureau base coat, walls), Boardman (bureau top coat), and Phelps Putty (numbers)

Marvelous mix-up
Who says dining room chairs need to match?
Here, seats in various shapes and sizes add
visual interest to a plain and simple space when
given a unifying coat of teal. Paint: Glidden's
Artisan (chairs) and Charade (walls)

Branching out
One quick way to freshen up an all-white
dresser: Paint a stencil of cornflower-blue blooms
across the drawer fronts. To avoid smudges,
apply only one color at a time and let it dry before
moving on to the next. Paint: Benjamin Moore's
White, Acorn, Weekend Getaway, and Blue
Bayou (dresser), and Soothing Green (walls)

Faux-aged armoire

→ We'll never tire of the sight of a proud piece of furniture displaying a timeworn finish. The trick to creating the look of a possession that's been handled by numerous owners is applying two (or more) layers of contrasting paint colors, then selectively sanding edges, corners, and contours that would naturally be exposed to wear.

The technique is a great way to break up the monolithic color of large pieces like this armoire, and it works especially well on furniture with moldings, aprons, relief, and other finish details. In other words: Yes to an ornate mirror frame, no to a Parsons table. Best of all, there's no need to prep the surface before you start painting. Any imperfections that could cause the paint you apply to fleck off will only add to its authentic character—faux as it may be.

time 4 hours over three days
difficulty Easy. If you can paint and sand wood, you can age a piece of furniture.

tools and materials

damp cloth to wipe down the interior

paint cup and **liners**

chip brushes Get one for the primer and each paint color.

medium-grit sanding sponge to remove layers of paint

latex primer-sealer to freshen up the interior

latex paint in two colors for the base and top coats (we used a satin sheen for both). Go for a light-dark contrast.

Paint: Behr's Sonata (base coat) and White Truffle (top coat)

1

Finish the interior

> There's no need for sanding, but you do want to wipe down the inside with a damp cloth to remove any dust and dirt. If it's grimy, break out the degreaser.

> In keeping with the distressed look intended for the exterior, you may want to patina the interior with primer, as we did to cover the original aqua. Using a disposable paint brush, cover the insides of the doors and cabinet with short, erratic brush strokes. Keep the brush pretty dry; you want the undercoat to peek through to give it a clean yet aged appearance.

2

Paint both coats

> Using a chip brush, paint the entire exterior with your base-coat color. Go with the grain, but don't be too fussy with the brush strokes.

> Once the first coat is dry, lightly apply the top-coat color. Be careful not to overload the brush.

3

Sand to finish

> Wait two days for the paint to dry. Take a medium-grit sanding sponge and scuff off paint at corners, edges, and details to let the underlayer of paint—or even a bit of raw wood—peek through. Continue until you achieve the distressed look you want.

> Unless the piece is going somewhere damp, such as a bathroom, skip any clear coat; any added sheen just takes away from the aged look.

Tip For a more nuanced look, you can sand all the way down to the original color—or even the bare wood.

◦IDEA FILE

Now that you know how to antique a piece
of furniture, have fun with all the ways
the technique can help you redefine a space.

Small scale, big impact
Not ready to try your hand at faux-aging a big bureau? Experiment with small items. Here,
a fancy plant stand and a simple mirror get a soft cottage look with two colors and some
sanding. Paint: Sherwin-Williams' Web Gray (plant-stand base coat), Undercool (plant-stand
top coat), Domino (mirror-frame base coat), and Alabaster (mirror-frame top coat)

Bold pairing
Two hot colors, red and yellow,
combine with visible brush
strokes on this humble hutch
to create a richly varied
surface that really stands out.
Paint: Olympic's Mustard
(base coat) and Apple-a-Day

Weathered effect
Give a brand-new
fireplace surround a
timeworn look with
soft green paint
rubbed off here and there
for a glimpse of brown
beneath. Paint: Glidden's
Old Cedar (base
coat) and Pastel Sage

Period standout
Painting a section of cabinets a separate color sets it off from the rest, and the aging effect with faux cherry peeking through makes it seem as if it could be an heirloom piece. Paint: Valspar's Autumn Russet (base coat) and Vintage Teal

Instant memories

Here, two classics come together for a winning combination: Jadeite green paint, reminiscent of dishware from the 1930s and 1940s, and a spindle-back Windsor chair. Paint: California Paints' Battle Spruce (base coat) and Venetian Glass

Deconstructed decor

When almost the entire top layer of paint is removed, a piece takes on an entirely different character—that of a rescued object filled with mystery and romance. Paint: C2 Paint's Sundown (base coat) and Tiger Lily

Aging gracefully

Cleverly painted distress lines and faux nicks give a new dresser a look of distinction. A faint spattering of dark paint creates the effect of wormholes—and the sense that this is a piece worth saving. Paint: Behr's Chai Spice (base coat), Willow Herb, and Carmel Woods (accents)

ALTERNATE TECHNIQUE:
WAX AND STEEL WOOL

> You can also faux-age new painted furniture with a candle, steel wool, and latex paint. This works especially well on pieces with detailed moldings, like this mirror.

> To do it, take a candle or piece of paraffin and run it over any high points and edges—natural places where paint might wear off with age (A).

> Paint the entire surface with a flat finish—any more sheen would look too new (B).

> Once the paint is dry, use fine steel wool to rub the surface. The paint will flake right off the waxed highlights, revealing the contrasting color underneath (C).

Paint: Valspar's Pale Ivory

Crackled kitchen island

→ Antique-furniture hounds spend years tracking down old pieces in hopes of finding one with that perfect painted patina, its cracked layers of color just oozing with charm. When a timeworn treasure does surface, immediately the musing begins: *How many times has it been painted? What kind of house did it come from? Whose idea was that mustard yellow?*

Today you can shortcut that journey considerably with a brush-on medium that shrinks your top coat to reveal a base color underneath. Crackle medium ages furniture right before your eyes. Which means you can create your own version of a piece's history, with colors of your choosing, whether you're aging one that's actually old or not. All that matters is the story you want to tell.

Paint: Benjamin Moore's Douglas Fern (base coat) and Autumn Purple (top coat)

time 2 hours over two days
difficulty Easy. The brush-on crackle medium does all the work for you.

tools and materials

damp sponge to clean off dirt

3-inch nylon-polyester paintbrushes Get two so that you'll have a clean one ready for the top coat.

cut bucket and **liners**

latex primer-sealer to create a good surface for the base coat

crackle medium We used Sherwin-Williams' Faux Impressions Crackle.

latex paint in two colors. Choose high-contrast colors for the most dramatic effect. For best results, be sure to use a flat finish for the top coat.

water-based polyurethane (optional) to clear coat and protect the crackle finish. Satin will look the best.

1

Prime, then paint the base coat

> No need for a lot of prep work here—surface imperfections are at the heart of this finish's charm. Just wipe it down with a wet sponge to remove surface dirt, and once it's dry, brush on a coat of primer. When the primed piece is dry, use a paintbrush to apply the color you want to show through in the crackle finish, brushing in the direction of the grain. Be sure to dab paint in the cracks and crevices of the furniture.

> Once you have an even coat, let it dry overnight.

2

Apply the crackle medium

> Using a clean paintbrush, apply a thick layer of crackle medium to all surfaces. Work from top to bottom in an orderly fashion so that you can keep track of where you've been, since the milky-looking coating goes on clear.

> Once you have an even coat, let it dry for at least an hour (but not more than 4 hours).

Tip Try a crackle finish on detailed shapes like lamp bases or turned table legs where other specialty paint techniques might feel daunting.

3

Paint the top coat

> Using a clean, dry brush, apply the top-coat color in a flat finish over all the painted surfaces. Even before you're finished with the entire piece, you'll see the top coat start to shrink up and reveal the color—and history—beneath.

> Let the piece cure overnight before using it.

> Finally, if you're crackling a surface that will get a lot of wear and tear—such as a tabletop, a chair seat, or a step stool—finish it with a satin clear coat to keep it from chipping. Otherwise, leave it as is for the most realistic aged finish.

Wood-grained bookcase

→ Traditional faux graining demands painstaking craftsmanship. Nowadays, however, if you don't wish to spend years mastering the art of making individual veins and knots with a tiny brush, you can pick up a wood-graining rocker at the home center that magically cuts a shapely heart grain into a layer of wet glaze. Add a paint comb and you can vary the pattern by creating knot-free "planks."

The result may not be as precise as the hand-painted approach, but it's no less amazing. Using a wood-graining rocker is a great way to evoke the real thing without trying to be overly serious—and to give an old piece of painted furniture entirely new character, like the bookcase here, for example. Best of all, it's a very quick process once you get the hang of it.

[ESSENTIAL TOOLS]
WOOD-GRAINING ROCKERS AND COMB
These inexpensive tools come in a variety of sizes from your local home center. Look for kits that combine different heads (and possibly a comb, too) so that you can vary the width and look of your "planks."

Paint: Benjamin Moore's Brown Horse (base coat) and White (glaze coat)

time 4 hours
difficulty Easy to moderate. Creating the wood grain couldn't be simpler, although you may need to experiment to achieve the overall pattern you want.

tools and materials
See what you need to prep your surface and paint the base coat, starting on page 134.

⅜-inch piece of MDF cut to size

two disposable cups and **wide-mouth container** to mix the paint and glaze

paint tray

9-inch roller frame with **½-inch nap roller cover** to apply the glaze

painting comb to cut in edges and blend the courses of grain

wood-graining rocker to create faux knots and veins

latex paint in two colors, one for the base and one to tint the glaze

clear acrylic glaze to create a semitranslucent, luminous top coat with an extended working time

See how to prep for and paint the **perfect base coat**, p.134.

1

Apply the glaze coat

> Instead of trying to faux-grain the inside edges of a bookcase, cut a back panel of ⅜-inch MDF to fit inside. Prime and paint it.

> Once the base coat is dry, mix equal parts acrylic glaze and paint, and pour into a paint tray.

> With the panel flat on a work surface, roll a 3-foot strip of glaze across the width of the panel along the top edge.

2

Cut in the grain

> Holding a paint comb at a 45-degree angle to the surface, cut in along the top edge of the panel. Pull the comb through the glaze in an uninterrupted motion to create veins running the width of the panel. This way, you don't have to line up your graining rocker with the edge of the panel for your first pass.

A

pro advice

INGRID LEESS, DECORATIVE PAINTER

"Once you get the knack of pulling
and rocking simultaneously,
you can add a twist to create an
undulation in the grain."

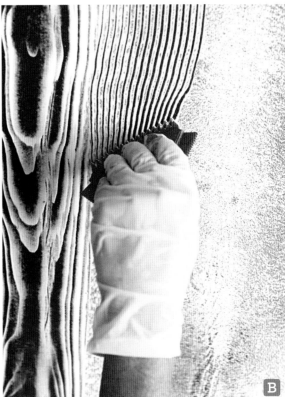

B

3

Create the planks

> Overlapping the combed border, set the heel of
the rocker on the far edge of the panel. Using one
smooth motion, pull the tool toward you while arching
your wrist to rock it and expose the full pattern to
the glaze (A). If the rocker tops out before the edge
of the panel, quickly cock your wrist and arch it
again as necessary until you finish pulling it across.

> Every so often, comb along the edge of a section
you've just completed to vary the look of your planks (B).

> To run the grain in the opposite direction,
flip the handle of the rocker so that you're starting
with the other side of the graining head.
Alternate how you use the rocker for consecutive
planks to create a more natural pattern.

Pickled oak bench

→ Pickling, bleaching, whitewash—they're all variations on the theme of treating light-colored woods, usually pine, oak, or ash, to make them appear even lighter, almost ethereal. This "limed" look stems from the 16th-century European practice of infusing wood with a paste of caustic lime to ward off insect infestation. Even then, it was appreciated for its decorative value.

Today you can just use leftover primer to create a simple pickling solution, or try one of the commercial pickling formulas out there. In either case, the process couldn't be simpler: Sand the wood, brush on the solution, wipe it off with a rag. The whitewash collects in the darker grain, creating a sort of sun-bleached negative of the natural wood for a weathered, driftwood look. Along with furniture like the red oak bench shown here, pickling is a great choice for pine floors, beadboard wainscot, and paneled shutters.

time About 5 hours over three days

difficulty Easy. The sanding takes a little elbow grease, but the pickling application is straightforward.

tools and materials

medium-grit and **fine-grit sanding sponges** to open the wood's pores and sand between clear coats

vacuum with brush attachment and **microfiber cloths** to remove sanding dust

two disposable cups and **wide-mouth container** to mix primer and water

4-inch nylon-polyester paintbrush to apply pickling solution

paint cup and **liners**

clean, dry rags

white latex primer-sealer to dilute with water to create a pickling paint (or use an off-the-shelf formula, such as Minwax's White Wash Pickling Stain)

2½-inch nylon-polyester paintbrush to apply clear coat

water-based polyurethane to clear coat and protect the pickling. Satin will look the best.

1

Prep the bench

> Using a medium-grit sanding sponge, scuff up all the surfaces to open the pores of the wood. Be sure to work with the grain.

> When you're finished, vacuum up any sawdust and wipe the surface with a reusable microfiber cloth.

2

Brush on pickling

> Mix 1 part white latex primer-sealer with 3 parts water. Using a 4-inch brush, paint on a patch of the pickling solution.

3

Rub it in, wipe it off

> Using a clean, dry rag, work the pickling solution into the wood by rubbing against the grain. Then, using a fresh rag, wipe with the grain to remove the excess and expose the grain.

> Repeat this sequence, working in patches to cover the entire bench evenly. Let dry overnight.

4

Apply clear coat

> Stir—but don't shake—a can of polyurethane clear coat. Pour some into a lined paint cup. Using a 2½-inch paintbrush, evenly coat the entire surface of the bench. Let dry for 24 hours.

> Sand lightly with a fine-grit sanding sponge. Wipe down the surface thoroughly with a dry rag and apply a second coat. If you plan to leave it on a covered porch, like we did, it will need a third coat, too.

Tip When pickling soft woods like pine, apply a water-based wood conditioner first, then sand lightly to allow the pickling to take evenly.

Spattered desk set

 With all due respect to Jackson Pollock, spattering is perhaps the simplest painting technique of all. It really is something your kid could do. That's not to trivialize its effect or usefulness: Spattering adds a modernist look wherever it's applied and can extend the aesthetic life of, say, worn laminate furniture, by way of camouflage.

All you do is load a brush and tap it against a stick to let fly with a spray of paint flecks. Still, easy as spattering is, achieving a uniform pattern of dots across a large surface—and keeping them from running together—can be tricky. That's why we chose a child's desk and chair to highlight the technique; it transforms the plain plywood furniture into something whimsical and original. And who knows, it may just inspire its little occupant to become a famous artist one day.

[ESSENTIAL TOOL]
SPATTER BRUSH
Any paintbrush that you can flick against a stick qualifies for this role. We used a natural pot scrubber after discovering that its fan of broom-root bristles neatly separates individual dots of paint.

Paint: Behr's Saffron (base coat) and Benjamin Moore's White (glaze coat)

time 6 hours including drying time
difficulty Easy but messy. Taking the the time to cover surrounding areas—and yourself— from flying paint is well worth it.

tools and materials
See what you need to prep the surfaces, starting on page 134.

3-inch nylon-polyester paintbrush for putting on the base coat

cut bucket and **liners**

eye protection, gloves, and **smock** to keep paint spray out of your eyes and off your skin

painter's tape and **plastic drop cloths** to mask off surfaces you don't want to spatter

two disposable cups and **wide-mouth container** for measuring and mixing paint and glaze

spatter brush with long, separated bristles

stick to tap the brush against

scrap cardboard for practicing your technique

latex paint in two colors. We used a satin formula for the base and for the paint to tint the glaze.

clear acrylic glaze to create semitranslucent, luminous spatters and extend the working time

See how to **prep surfaces** for paint, page 134.

1

Paint the base coat

> When the primed surfaces are dry, brush on the base coat, working along the length of the piece of furniture. Let dry.

> Apply a second coat if needed.

> Use plastic drop cloths and tape to cover any surfaces that won't be spattered, such as the base and sides of our chair.

A

B

2

Mix the paint and glaze, dip the brush

> In a wide-mouth mixing container, combine equal parts clear acrylic glaze and top-coat color (A). Stir the mixture, which should be creamy and luminous.

> Load the spatter brush by dipping just the bristle tips in the mixture (B).

Tip Use spent sanding sponges to prop up and steady any furniture you paint so that it won't stick to your work surface.

3

Start spattering

> Test your technique on cardboard before moving on to your furniture pieces.

> Tap the brush lightly against a firmly held stick. Try to maintain the same pressure and cadence as you spatter one entire surface. Find a rhythm, and stick to it.

> If you don't like the emerging pattern, simply wipe off the glaze with a wet rag and try again when the surface dries.

> Once you spatter one side to your satisfaction, let it dry before turning the piece and spattering another surface.

Tip Move closer to the surface for bigger spatters and farther away for smaller ones.

Herringbone tabletop

→ If you like the ordered feel of geometric lines, you'll love what a paint comb can do for you. It offers an expedient way to work a pattern of evenly spaced parallel stripes into glaze. How you apply them—in squiggles, chevrons, a crisscrossing design—is up to you.

We blocked out a bright, bold herringbone on the old laminated table here to inject some eye-opening zing into a breakfast nook. It's a lively twist on an age-old pattern and much easier to execute than it might seem. Just tape off rows and drag a comb diagonally across half of them in one direction, then half in the other.

time 4 hours over three days

difficulty Moderate. You have to account for drying time for three coats, but the taping and combing is straightforward.

tools and materials
See what you need to prep your surface and paint the base coat, starting on page 134.

tape measure and **pencil**

3-inch painter's tape to mask off the herringbone stripes

plastic putty knife to seal edges of tape, plus an extra if you're cutting one up to make the comb

mini roller and **foam cover**

mini roller paint tray

paint comb

latex paint in two colors, one for the base coat and one to tint the glaze coat

clear acrylic glaze to create a semitranslucent, luminous top coat with an extended working time

[ESSENTIAL TOOL]
PAINT COMB
You can buy a comb, or, for a more homespun look, craft your own by snipping teeth out of a plastic lid or putty knife.

Paint: Behr's Silver Drop (base coat), and Glidden's Sunny (glaze coat)

See how to prep for and paint the **perfect base coat,** page 134.

1
Find the center

> Once the base coat is dry, find and mark the centerpoint of your surface. To do that on a round table like this one, hook the tape measure to one edge, extend it fully across the tabletop, and sweep it like a pendulum to locate the longest cross section: the diameter. Divide that number in half and mark the centerpoint on the table surface.

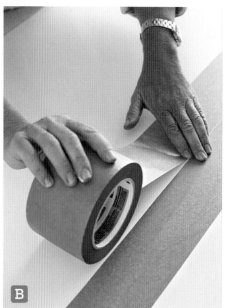

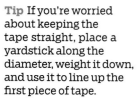

Tip If you're worried about keeping the tape straight, place a yardstick along the diameter, weight it down, and use it to line up the first piece of tape.

2
Set the row spacing

> Use the centerpoint to place your first piece of tape, lining up one edge along the diameter and keeping it taut (A). The ends of the tape can overlap the lip of the table by a few inches. Run a second piece of tape alongside the first—it doesn't matter to which side (B). Then add a third piece right alongside that one (C). The second piece will serve as a spacer to keep an even distance between each row of tape.

3

Tape the first series of rows

> Remove the middle piece of tape: the spacer (A). Transfer it to the outside of the last piece laid down (B). Align it edge to edge, and pat it down lightly to the surface.

> Now, for the third row, affix another piece along the exposed edge of the spacer. Repeat this process of leapfrogging the spacer and affixing new rows until the entire surface is covered. You should have an even series of alternating stripes.

4

Make the combing tool (optional)

> If you want to make your own tool, it's easy with a plastic putty knife. Using a pair of sharp scissors, cut V-shaped notches into the tip of the knife to clip out teeth. The wider the putty knife, the fewer passes you'll have to make through the glaze.

Tip Reserve another plastic putty knife to adhere the tape to the table. Run the smooth blade along the tape's edges to ensure paint doesn't bleed underneath.

5

Apply the glaze

> Mix equal parts clear acrylic glaze and paint, then pour into a mini roller tray.

> Using a small foam roller, apply the tinted glaze to the open areas between the taped lines. Cover every bit of the exposed surface with a thick coat.

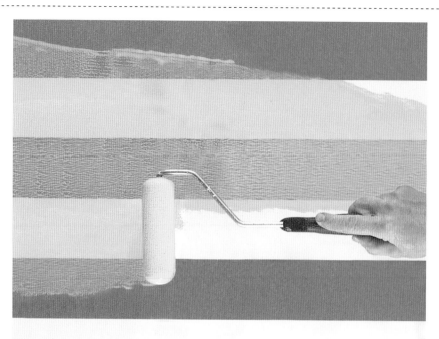

Tip It's always best to roll with the direction of the tape, lest you push paint beneath its edges by coming at them from a 90-degree angle.

6

Comb the surface

> Set your comb at a 45-degree angle to the stripes and pull it steadily across the surface, cutting through the glaze. Keeping the comb at a shallow angle to the surface will help prevent scraping up the tape.

> On the second pass, overlap several teeth of the comb with the first to keep the grooves parallel. Repeat across the entire surface.

> If you make a mistake, just reroll and redo.

7

Tape stripes for the second coat

> Remove the tape while the glaze is still tacky to keep from peeling it off. Pull the tape at a diagonal (A).

> Let the glaze dry, which could take a day, depending on temperature and humidity.

> Once dry, cover the stripes with painter's tape (B). Press the edges down with a plastic putty knife.

A

B

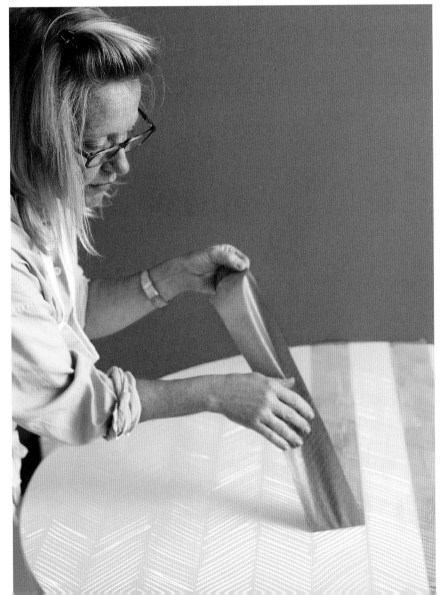

8

Roll and comb the second set of stripes

> Repeat Steps 5 and 6, combing the glaze at a 90-degree angle to the first set of stripes to create the herrringbone pattern.

> Remove the tape while the glaze is still tacky.

CHAPTER 5

Floors

Paint has embellished wood floors since colonial times, when artisans used color to create mock marble and other fancy effects. Today, painting floors still typically involves a base coat topped with a design in a contrasting color or two. That's a good option when the alternative is refinishing or replacing worn floorboards. If the wood is too nice to hide under a blanket of paint—but feels too bare left alone—there are also designs that let the natural wood shine through. Either way, painting the floor is a great way to personalize your space.

Paint: Benjamin Moore's
Black Impervo

Classic checkerboard

 A two-tone geometric pattern of squares turned on the diagonal is a traditional design that works in a wide variety of rooms. Often seen in foyers to mimic the look of tile, its slanting lines can visually expand a small space. In a hard-working laundry room or kitchen, it's a good way to introduce an energizing dose of color and the finished look of a rug without the inherent vulnerability to spills and stains. High-gloss paint adds durability; semigloss can be used to tone down the sheen.

As with any paint job, preparation is key. So start with a freshly cleaned floor ready to be scuff-sanded. When it comes to color choices, your mind's eye is the limit. A good starting point is to pair up colors based on how you want the space to feel: calming (pastels), classic (neutrals), or just plain fun (brights).

Paint: Valspar's Clean White (base coat), Old Gold 6 (checks), and Sun Hat (walls)

time 3 hours a day over three days
difficulty Easy to moderate. Calculating the pattern requires some math and taping it some precision, but the painting is basic.

tools and materials

pole sander with **150-grit silicon-carbide sandpaper** and **medium-grit sanding sponge** to prep wood floor

damp sponge

plastic sheeting

paint tray and **liners**

9-inch roller frame with **½-inch nap roller cover** and **extension pole**

ruler or **yardstick** and **pencil**

framing square

delicate-adhesion painter's tape It won't pull up the base coat when removed.

putty knife

2½-inch angled nylon-polyester paintbrush

3-inch mini roller frame and **foam cover**

acrylic porch and floor enamel that stands up to foot traffic and scuffs. One gallon covers about 400 square feet; you'll need enough base color for two coats and enough pattern color to cover half the floor with two coats.

water-based polyurethane (optional) for a top coat with added durability. Satin finish will look best.

1

Prep the base

> Using a pole sander, gently rough up the floor finish and level any high spots from the previous finish. For edges and corners, use a sanding sponge.

> Wipe the floor clean with a damp sponge and allow it to dry. Tape an apron of plastic sheeting to the bottom of doors to prevent dust from blowing in and ruining the paint finish while it's wet.

2

Paint the base coat

> Use a 2½-inch paintbrush to cut in around the edges of the floor with the base color.

> With the paint roller attached to an extension pole, coat the entire field, starting opposite a door so that you can paint yourself out of the room.

> Let the paint dry overnight before laying out the pattern and applying the second color.

A

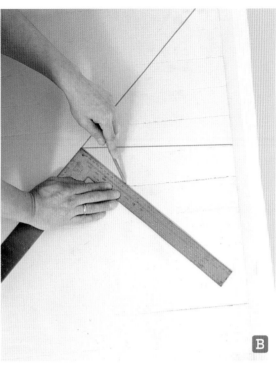

B

3

Measure and mark the pattern

> The pattern will look best if it ends in perfect half-square triangles at the most visible walls, so figure out which wall is least visible and start measuring on the opposite side of the room.

> Estimate the number of squares you want to fit across the middle wall of the three most visible walls. Divide the length of the wall by the number of squares. Mark off the wall from corner to corner with this measurement (A).

> Mark the center point between the marks for the first square and note the distance from there to the corner.

> Using a framing square, draw a perpendicular reference line out from the center point, making it the same length as the distance to the corner. Then connect the corner to the end of the reference line. This is one side of the first square (B).

> Using a ruler or yardstick, extend the reference line out into the room. Mark the entire line at intervals to match the length of one side of each pattern square.

> Using a framing square as a right-angle guide, complete the squares at each mark (C). Double-check your layout by making sure you connect back to the marks on the first wall.

C

4

Tape the checkerboard

> With the pattern drawn, use painter's tape to X out the squares you intend to leave the base color. Then tape along the outside edges of the unmarked squares.

> Keep in mind that the painter's tape outlines the box you're painting, so it will fall on alternating sides of the grid lines (A).

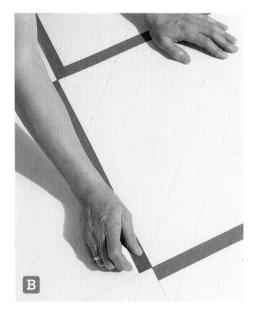

> Seal the tape to the floor by hand, then pull a putty-knife blade over the tape to remove air bubbles and prevent paint from bleeding underneath and onto the lighter-colored squares (B).

> Cut each piece of tape cleanly by tearing it against a putty knife. Hold the blade on the tape and rip away from the knife to execute a perfect cut and make sharp corners for each square (C). Continue taping until all the unmarked squares are outlined.

Tip Clean up pencil marks with a damp sponge instead of an eraser, which can damage the freshly painted base coat.

5
Paint the pattern

> Using a sanding sponge, lightly sand the squares to be painted and wipe them clean.

> Using a 2½-inch angled paintbrush, cut in along the edges of the squares. Start each stroke on the tape, and pull it onto the square so that the color doesn't push under the tape's edge. Coat the entire perimeter of the square this way.

> While the edges are still wet, fill in the field using a mini roller. Roll the paint on in the same direction as the floorboards.

> Continue painting the squares in this manner until the floor is finished. Clean up any drips or mistakes by wiping them up with a damp rag while they're still wet.

6
Finish up

> Remove the tape before the paint dries so that it doesn't pull up any color with it. Peel the tape up and away from the paint at an angle to leave a clean edge.

> Acrylic porch and floor paint is very durable, but for high-traffic areas consider topping the floor with a coat of water-based polyurethane. After the paint has dried for a full day, use a roller to apply the finish evenly across the floor. If you plan to add a second coat, lightly sand the first coat before putting the second one down.

Tip The higher the gloss on paint or polyurethane, the more durable it is. If you want the resilience of high gloss without the shine, put on a top coat of satin polyurethane to tone down the gloss.

○IDEA FILE

A checkerboard may be a classic pattern for a painted floor, but that doesn't mean it has to look staid. Here, some updated interpretations

Tile-look design
Checks in crisp blue and white liven up a vintage-look bath. Paint: Valspar's Clean White (checks, walls), Classic Blue (checks), and Beach House (tub surround)

Light and bright
The subtle contrast in this pale yellow-and-white checkerboard floor magnifies the sun-filled effect in this all-white break-fast nook. Paint: Sherwin-Williams' Pearl Onion (checks, walls), Narcissus (checks), Restful (table), and Citrine (chair)

Sea-glass colors

Lively checks of turquoise and lime outlined in denim blue create a summerhouse vibe all year long. Paint: Benjamin Moore's Skylark Song and Fun in the Sun (checks), Stillwater (thin outlines), Super White (walls), and Neon (cabinet)

The warmth of wood

Brown squares set off caramel-color wood grain in this design, an unexpectedly dressy look in a country bedroom. Paint: Olympic's Olive Wood (floor) and Cookie Crumb (walls)

Carpet squares

The hunter-green-and-white checkerboard's thick border with a slim sage-colored accent makes this colorful kitchen feel fully furnished. Paint: Benjamin Moore's Holiday Wreath and Oxford White (checks), Greenwich Village (accent border), Chameleon (walls), and Mediterranean Spice (cabinets)

Framed medallion

→ When two types of flooring meet, a painted pattern can ease the transition. Here, an existing oak floor abuts an addition's heart-pine boards, which run perpendicular to the oak. The open cloverleaf design, squared off and anchored by painted borders and solid circles at the center and four corners, helps conceal the inconsistencies. It also softens the area's angles and echoes the arched passageway.

Though it fits neatly in this symmetrical spot, the design can also be altered to suit different spaces. Change the borders to create a wider or narrower frame. A row of smaller cloverleaf designs would work equally well in a longer, rectangular area. Let your space's parameters—and your imagination—be your guide. One last note: You'll be working with oil-based paint here, so your clean-up will require mineral spirits.

time Two days
difficulty Moderate. Just don't let yourself say, "I can't draw a circle."

tools and materials

scrap paper and **pencil** to sketch your design

medium-grit sanding sponge to prep the floor

ruler or **yardstick**

small nail and **nylon string** to make a compass

mineral spirits and **rag**

2-inch natural-bristle paintbrush

3-inch chip brush for the polyurethane

interior oil paint in eggshell. One gallon is plenty; for a smaller medallion, you may get away with just a quart.

oil-based polyurethane for a top coat with added durability. Satin finish will look best.

Paint: Pratt & Lambert's Obsidian

1

Figure out your design

> Measure the area to cover, and draw a pattern to scale on paper, adjusting proportions to make a cloverleaf within a square. Here, the center dot, 2 feet across, is framed by open "leaves" of a similar size. Solid 10-inch circles ground the design at the four corners. As shown on the previous page, placing the 5-foot square inside a 6-by-9-foot area allows for an interesting rectangular border.

2

Mark the pattern

> Rough up the floor with a medium-grit sanding sponge.

> Using a pencil and yardstick, mark off the 5-foot-square border.

> Make a compass with a small nail, a nylon string, and a pencil. Tap the nail into the center point of the medallion and draw the diameter of the largest circle; it will touch the painted border. Then draw the inside border of that circle, 1½ inches smaller. Draw the 2-foot-diameter center circle (A), then the smaller corner circles.

> Divide up the remaining space to determine the size of the four open leaves, which will have 1½-inch-wide outlines that touch the largest circle. Using the string compass, draw the outside lines of each leaf, then the inside lines (B).

3

Paint the medallion

> Working your way out from the center, use a small paintbrush and oil-based paint to fill in the solid center circle (A). Then fill in the outlines of the four leaves and the large open circle (B). Paint the four solid corner circles and thick border last.

> Keep mineral spirits and a rag handy to fix any slipups.

4

Finish up

> Allow the paint to dry overnight. Finish with a coat of satin polyurethane. Let dry overnight; sand lightly, vacuum, then apply a second coat.

pro advice   BRIAN CARTER, DECORATIVE PAINTER

"Don't obsess about perfection—no one is going to get down on the floor and look at your painting that closely. Ditto for any small scratches and chips later on. They give a painted floor patina, a lived-in look."

IDEA FILE:
MORE PAINTED FLOORS

Ever think there's a wide-open canvas right at your feet? Consider adding one of these graphic accents

High-contrast border
Medallions of bright white stand out against this ebonized oak floor. Using a stencil to add a border is a great way to define a space, such as a dining area, in an open-plan interior. Paint: Valspar's Clean White

Diamonds and gold
Dots of color bring out the undertones of warm oak floorboards and give the framed latticework design a lift. Paint: Benjamin Moore's Black and Hawthorne Yellow

Colorful patchwork
Crisp white stenciled petals pop against a random checkerboard of repeating colors. Paint: Behr's Camembert (petal outlines), Summer Field, Blue Luxury, Briquette, Emerald Coast, and Licorice Stick

Gingham checks
To establish a cohesive look, take inspiration for a painted floor from fabric in the room. In this bedroom, a favorite wing chair's yellow-plaid fabric is echoed in the floor pattern. Paint: Behr's Cotton Fluff (base coat) and California Dreaming

Shipshape
This painted wood floor's nautical palette puts a playful spin on traditional boat decking. The compass medallion provides a dramatic anchor for a spiral staircase. Paint: Pratt & Lambert's Cornflower, Captivating, and Super One Coat Interior

Outlined diamonds
A gridlike pattern
of black squares
turned on end has an
invigorating, off-kilter
effect, overlaid on top
of stained floorboards.
Paint: Benjamin Moore's
Midnight Oil (dots)

Faux bois
A hand-painted woodgrain
pattern in graphic black-and-
white takes these traditional
wood floors from standard to
striking. Paint: Behr's
Polar Bear and Black Sable

○IDEA FILE: STAIRCASES

Now that you've got the hang of painting underfoot, why not take your skills vertical? A staircase is a great place to add some surprising color and pattern

Crisp contrast
A bright red stenciled motif on the risers in the same shade as the treads perk up this otherwise white set of stairs. Paint: Ralph Lauren Paint's Tack Room White and Mai Tai Red

Send a message
Use a few choice stenciled-on words to beckon kids, overnight guests, or your own sleepy self to bed. Paint: Glidden's Valentine Pink and Antique White

Reverse runner
Rather than a faux carpet flowing down the center, this stenciled border wraps just the edges of the treads and risers, letting the weathered wood steps show through. Paint: Ralph Lauren Paint's Crescent Moon

How to paint stairs

1_ **Lay a good foundation.** Scuff-sand an existing coat of varnish or polyurethane to provide a good surface for the paint to grip. If the stairs are unfinished wood, add a coat of primer-sealer, which can be tinted to match the color of your base coat. Let it sit for a few days to fully cure.

2_ **Paint your base coat.** Be sure to clean the stairs before you start. Then vacuum and dust with a tack cloth. Use painter's tape to mark the edges. If you're painting the entire set of stairs (as shown on this page), work from top to bottom with a mini roller or a 2½-inch paint-brush. If the staircase cannot be closed to traffic, paint every other stair. Oil paint will give you a harder surface, but you can use water-based porch and floor enamel as well. Use two coats for the base. Allow 18 to 20 hours of drying time between each coat.

3_ **Lay out the design.** Draw your design with a watercolor pencil. It has a softer tip than a lead pencil, so it won't dent the wood, and is available in a variety of colors. Tape off the shapes one color at a time with delicate-adhesion painter's tape that resists bleeding. Press down the edges with a plastic putty knife.

4_ **Paint the design.** Paint shapes with a stiff, flattop stencil brush using a dabbing motion. Paint in short runs—five or six stairs at a time—so that you can remove the tape before the paint dries. Gently remove tape while the paint is still tacky, and clean up any jagged edges with a moist cotton swab.

5_ **Add a clear coat.** To keep your painted stairs looking good for the long haul, consider finishing them with a coat of polyurethane. Or use traditional shellac for an antiqued amber sheen.

Ruglike stripes
Get the traditional look of a stair runner—without the expense—by painting one on. Here, the whole staircase was given a coat of caramel, then the center was painted to match the walls. A pair of thin red stripes on both sides completes the illusion. Paint: Valspar's Warm Buff (base coat), Kabuki Clay, and Quite Red

Credits

Cover: (clockwise from top) Wendell T. Webber; Deborah Whitlaw Llewellyn; Kolin Smith; Wendell T. Webber

Back Cover: (top) Paul Raeside/Livingetc/IPC Images; (middle) Wendell T. Webber; (bottom) Matthew Benson

p. 1: Ted Morrison

pp. 2–3: (clockwise from top left) Deborah Whitlaw Llewellyn; Nathan Kirkman; Wendell T. Webber (2); Darren Setlow/Built Images/Alamy; Bieke Claessens/Getty Images

p. 4: (top) Kolin Smith; (middle) Anthony Tieuli; (bottom) Carl Tremblay

p. 5: (left) Wendell T. Webber; (right) Deborah Whitlaw Llewellyn

p. 7: Darrin Haddad

p. 8: Darrin Haddad (3); (carriers) Wendell T. Webber

p. 9: (top) Courtesy of American Antiquarian Society of Worcester; (bottom) Courtesy of Mount Vernon

p. 10: Darrin Haddad

p. 11: Courtesy of Old Sturbridge

p. 13: Kenneth Chen

p. 14: Ted Morrison

p. 15: (clockwise from top left) David Prince; Joshua McHugh; Tria Giovan; Ted Morrison; Andre Baranowski

p. 16: (clockwise from left) Laura Moss; Wendell T. Webber (2)

p. 17: (left) Dan Duchars/IPC Images; (right) Don Penny/Time Inc. Digital Studio

p. 18: Ted Morrison; (tip) Brian Wilder

p. 19: (clockwise from bottom left) Keate; Erika Larsen; Wendell T. Webber; Ted Morrison (3)

p. 20: (clockwise from top left) Wendell T. Webber; Ted Morrison (4); Anthony Tieuli; Ted Morrison (2)

p. 21: (left 3) Ted Morrison; (right 4) Chris Buck

p. 22: Ted Morrison

p. 23: Ted Morrison; (pro advice) Anthony Tieuli; (roller pan) Don Penny/Time Inc. Digital Studio

p. 24: Ted Morrison; (pro advice) Kolin Smith

p. 25: Ted Morrison

p. 26: Virgil Bastos/Time Inc. Digital Studio

p. 27: Ted Morrison

p. 28: Ted Morrison

p. 29: (paint cans) Ted Morrison; (swatches) Don Penny/Time Inc. Digital Studio

p. 30: Susan Seubert

p. 31: (clockwise from top right) Mark Scott/IPC Images; Lizzie Orme/IPC Images; Mark Lohman

p. 32: (clockwise from top right) Nathan Kirkman; Mark Scott/IPC Images; Steve Wilson

p. 33: (clockwise from top) Alex Hayden; Mark Scott/IPC Images; Mark Lohman

p. 34: (clockwise from top) Adrian Briscoe/IPC Images; Casey Sills; Roger Davies

p. 35: (clockwise from top right) Laura Moss; Tim Young/IPC Images; Mark Lund

p. 36: (clockwise from left) Anthony Tieuli; Oliver Gordon/Ideal Home/IPC Images; Chris Everard/Homes & Gardens/IPC Images

p. 37: (clockwise from top left) Deborah Whitlaw Llewellyn; Kenneth Chen; Mark Lohman

p. 38: Alex Hayden

p. 39: (top) Mark Lohman; (bottom) Wendell T. Webber

p. 40: (clockwise from top left) Eric Roth; David Prince; Susan Seubert; Laura Moss

p. 41: Tria Giovan

p. 42: Mark Scott/Ideal Home/IPC Images

p. 43: Matthew Benson

p. 44: Matthew Benson

p. 45: Jürgen Frank

p. 47: Tom Leighton/Homes & Gardens/IPC Images

pp. 48–57: Kolin Smith

p. 58: (left) Dan Duchars/Red Cover/Alamy; (right) Bieke Claessens/Getty Images

p. 59: Alise O'Brien

p. 60: Paul Raeside/Livingetc/IPC Images

p. 61: (left) Chris Everard/Homes & Gardens/IPC Images; (right) Russell Sadur/IPC Images

p. 62: (left) Jessie Walker/Cornerhouse Stock; (right) Richard Powers/Arcaid/Corbis

p. 63: (top) Adobe/Beateworks/Corbis; (bottom) Tim Street-Porter/Beateworks/Corbis

pp. 64–67: Wendell T. Webber

pp. 69–71: Deborah Whitlaw Llewellyn

p. 72: (left) Graeme Ainscough/IPC Images; (right) Dominic Blackmore/IPC Images

p. 73: Stewart Grant/ESS/IPC Images (2)

pp. 75–77: Kolin Smith

p. 78: (bottom left) Ted Morrison; (right) Wendell T. Webber

p. 79: Wendell T. Webber

p. 80: Wendell T. Webber

p. 81: (clockwise from top left) Ted Morrison; Wendell T. Webber (2)

p. 82: Ted Morrison

pp. 83–87: Kolin Smith

p. 88: (top) Russell Sadur/IPC Images; (bottom) Tom Leighton/IPC Images

Paint: Behr's Pale Sky (walls) and Snow fall (trim)

Paint: Olympic's Forsythia Blossom (cabinets) and Bewitched (island)

p. 89: (left) Adrian Briscoe/ESS/IPC Images; (right) Lucy Pope/Homes & Gardens/IPC Images

p. 90: (left) Andrew Cameron/IPC Images; (right) Mel Yates/Ideal Home/IPC Media

p. 91: Caroline Arber/Homes & Gardens/IPC Images

p. 92: Tom Leighton/IPC Images

p. 93: Mel Yates/Ideal Home/ IPC Images

p. 94: Ted Morrison

pp. 95–97: Wendell T. Webber

pp. 99–103, 104–107: Deborah Whitlaw Llewellyn

p. 108: Ted Morrison

p. 110: (illustration: floral pattern) Gregory Nemec

pp. 109–111 Deborah Whitlaw Llewellyn

p. 113: Bruce Buck

p. 115: Wendell T. Webber

p. 116: Mark Weiss

p. 117: (left) Allison Dinner; (right) Mr. P. Andrew Bilbao

p. 118: (bottom) Matthew Benson; (top) Kolin Smith

p. 119: (clockwise from bottom right) Spike Powell/IPC Images; Bruce Buck (2)

p. 120: Chris Everard/Livingetc/ IPC Images

p. 121: (top) Keller & Keller; (bottom) Eric Piasecki; (illustrations: windows) Gregory Nemec

p. 123: (top) Susan Gilmore; (bottom) Nathan Kirkman

p. 124: Tria Giovan

p. 125: (top) Josh McHugh; (bottom) Laura Moss

p. 126: (illustrations: doors) Gregory Nemec

p. 127: (left) Chris Everard/IPC Images; (right) Mel Yates/Livingetc/ IPC Images

p. 128: (left) Jamie Mason/Ideal Home/IPC Images; (right) Tom Leighton/Livingetc/IPC Images

p. 129: Eric Piasecki

p. 130: Mark Lohman

p. 131: (clockwise from left) Abode/ Beateworks/Corbis; Mark Scott/ Ideal Home/IPC Images; Wendell T. Webber

p. 133: Alex Hayden

pp. 134–137: Kolin Smith

p. 138: Julian Wass

p. 139: John Granen

p. 140: (top) Alex Hayden; (bottom) Deborah Whitlaw Llewellyn

p. 141: Matthew Millman

p. 142: Bruce Buck (2)

p. 143: Joe Standart

p. 144: (left) Nathan Kirkman; (right) Julian Wass

p. 145: Mark Lohman

p. 146: (left) Chris Everard/ Homes & Gardens/IPC Images; (right) Bruce Buck

p. 147: David Prince

p. 148: (left) Alex Hayden; (right) John Granen

p. 149: Joshua McHugh

p. 150: (left) Chris Everard/Homes & Gardens/IPC Images; (right) Mel Yates/Livingetc/IPC Images

p. 151: Polly Wreford/Homes & Gardens/IPC Images (2)

p. 152: (left) Catherine Gratwicke/ Livingetc/IPC Images; (right) Peter Tilley/IPC Images

p. 153: (top) Rebecca Duke/ Livingetc/IPC Images; (bottom) Tim Young/Ideal Home/IPC Images

pp. 155–157: Wendell T. Webber

p. 158: (left) Brent Darby/Country Homes & Interiors/IPC Images; (right) Elizabeth Whiting & Associates/Alamy

p. 159: (left) Robert Kent; (right) Jessie Walker/Cornerhouse Stock

p. 160: (clockwise from left) James Gardiner/Essentials/IPC Images;

Debi Treloar/IPC Images; Alun Callender/IPC Images

p. 161: Mark Scott/Essentials/ IPC Images (4)

pp. 163–183: Wendell T. Webber

p. 185: Deborah Whitlaw Llewellyn

pp. 187–191: Kolin Smith

p. 192: (left) Erik Johnson; (right) Eric Roth

p. 193: (clockwise from top left) Richard Leo Johnson; Robbie Caponetto; Deborah Whitlaw Llewellyn

pp. 195–197: Deborah Whitlaw Llewellyn

p. 198: (left) Deborah Whitlaw Llewellyn; (right) James Merrell/ Livingetc/IPC Images

p. 199: Darren Setlow/Built Images/ Alamy

p. 200: (left) Jean Allsopp; (right) J. Savage Gibson

p. 201: (left) Huntley Hedworth/Red Cover; (right) William Abranowicz

p. 202: (clockwise from left) Neil Davis/EWA; Niall McDiarmid/Alamy; Spike Powell/Country Homes & Interiors/IPC Images

p. 203: Nathan Kirkman

p. 204: Alise O'Brien

p. 205: Nathan Kirkman

Index

ISBN-10: 0-8487-3411-4
ISBN-13: 978-0-8487-3411-4
Library of Congress Control Number: 2009941791

Printed in the United States of America
First Printing 2011

Oxmoor House
VP, Publishing Director: Jim Childs
Editorial Director: Susan Payne Dobbs
Brand Manager: Fonda Hitchcock
Managing Editor: Laurie S. Herr

This Old House
Weekend Remodels: Paint Ideas & Projects
Design Director: Hylah Hill
Editor: Kathryn Keller
Contributing Editors: Thomas Baker, Deborah Baldwin, Jessica Dodell-Feder, Eric Hagerman, Deborah Snoonian
Contributing Art Director: Bess Yoham
Photo Editor: Denise Sfraga
Editorial Operations Director: Carolyn Blackmar
Editorial Production Manager: Yoshiko Taniguchi-Canada
Copy Editor: Alan Lockwood
Research Editors: Ambrose Martos, Mark Powers
Proofreader: Timothy E. Pitt
Indexer: Marjorie Joy
Prepress Coordinator: Al Rufino
Design and Prepress Manager: Ann-Michelle Gallero
Book Production Manager: Susan Chodakiewicz

Our thanks to the Rohm and Haas Paint Quality Institute (paintquality.com)

To order additional publications, call 1-800-765-6400 or 1-800-491-0551.

For more books to enrich your life, visit oxmoorhouse.com.

To subscribe to *This Old House* magazine, go to thisoldhouse.com/customerservice or call 1-800-898-7237.

This Old House Magazine
Editor: Scott Omelianuk
Publisher: Charles R. Kammerer

EDITORIAL
Deputy Editor: Kathryn Keller
Editorial Operations Director: Carolyn Blackmar
Building Technology Editor: Thomas Baker
Design Editor: Colette Scanlon
Features Editor: Amy R. Hughes
Articles Editor: Deborah Baldwin
Senior Editor: Deborah Snoonian
Senior Technical Editor: Mark Powers
Staff Editor: Jessica Dodell-Feder
Associate Editors: Keith Pandolfi, Natalie Rodriguez
Assistant Editors: Sal Vaglica, Jennifer Stimpson
Copy Chief: Timothy E. Pitt
Deputy Copy Chief: Leslie Monthan
Senior Contributors: Mark Feirer, Eric Hagerman
**Editorial Assistant
and Assistant to the Editor:** Danielle Blundell

ART
Design Director: Hylah Hill
Photo Editor: Denise Sfraga
Deputy Art Director: Douglas Adams
Associate Art Director: Leslie Steiger
Associate Photo Editor: Allison Chin
Art/Online Assistant: Robert Hardin
Editorial Production Manager: Yoshiko Taniguchi-Canada

ONLINE
Online Editor: Alexandra Bandon
Web Designer: Bill Mazza
Assistant Editor: Tabitha Sukhai
Contributing Producer: Amanda Keiser

EDITORIAL BOARD
Master Carpenter: Norm Abram
General Contractor: Tom Silva
Plumbing and Heating Expert: Richard Trethewey
Landscape Contractor: Roger Cook
Host: Kevin O'Connor

This Old House Ventures Inc.
President: John L. Brown